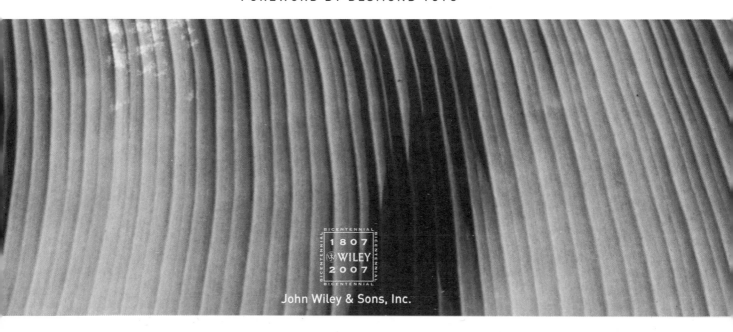

DISCOVERY OF A CONTINENT

FOODS, FLAVORS, AND INSPIRATIONS FROM AFRICA

MARCUS SAMUELSSON

WITH HEIDI SACKO WALTERS

PHOTOGRAPHS BY GEDIYON KIFLE

FOREWORD BY DESMOND TUTU

BICENTENNIAL
1807
WILEY
2007
BICENTENNIAL

John Wiley & Sons, Inc.

LIBRARY OF CONGRESS CATALOGING-IN-PUBLICATION DATA:

Samuelsson, Marcus.

Discovery of a continent: foods, flavors, and inspirations from Africa / Marcus Samuelsson, with Heidi Sacko Walters ; photographs by Gediyon Kifle ; foreword by Desmond Tutu. – Starbucks custom version.

p. cm.

Includes index.

ISBN 978-0-470-17325-1 (pbk.)

1. Cookery, African. I. Walters, Heidi Sacko. II. Title.

TX725.A4S26 2007

641.596–dc22

2007013698

Printed in China

10 9 8 7 6 5 4 3 2 1

Wiley Bicentennial Logo:
Richard J. Pacifico

Design by Vertigo Design
NYC

CONTENTS

W HEN I THINK OF AFRICA AND ITS CUISINE, THE CREATION STORY COMES TO MIND. Most of us are familiar with the first few chapters of Genesis in the Bible. Isn't there a veritable explosion of creativity? God, it could be said, went on a real spree, almost, one might say, an orgy of creativity—where there was chaos, darkness, and disorder, now there was order, cosmos, and light, and what a kaleidoscope of diversity. There were trees, stars, a sun and moon, rivers and seas, fish, fowl, and birds and animals, not just one sort but a whole range of different animals; giraffes, elephants, lions, tigers, sheep, and we could go on and on, and then there was Adam. He was all by himself and God saw that it was not good for man to be alone. And then we have that lovely story of how Eve came about.

We say in Africa that a person is a person through other persons. A solitary human being is a contradiction in terms. We are made for togetherness, for friendship, for fellowship. Food is a part of that fellowship. We are created to live in a delicate network of interdependence and we are different precisely in order to know our need of one another. Diversity, difference is the essence of who we are. Nowhere is that diversity and sense of fellowship more apparent than on the continent of Africa, as expressed through its many varied cuisines and tradition of hospitality.

I come from South Africa, a beautiful land richly endowed by God with wonderful natural resources, wide expanses, rolling mountains, singing birds, bright shining stars out of blue skies, with radiant sunshine, golden sunshine. This land, which carried the opprobrium of the world for its vicious apartheid policy, is home to a vast array of people and thus cuisines. The land here is fertile and bears everything from the grapes that make the famed wine—pinotage—to the corn that is the base to mealie pap, to the spices that comprise Indian and Cape Malay cuisine. I mention South Africa because it is the land I know best and because it is a microcosm of the world and an example of what is to be found in other lands in differing degrees; a fantastic array of remarkable difference and diversity, different languages, different cultures, different ethnicities, different this, different that. We are indeed the rainbow people of God.

I commend Marcus for recognizing the culinary gifts that Africa offers and for undertaking the huge and important task of documenting its cuisine and sharing it with the world so that people everywhere can experience the cuisine and hospitality of this stunning continent and its rainbow nations. His work pays homage to Africa's humanity. Let us break bread together and celebrate our diversity.

Archbishop Desmond Tutu

COFFEE IS CULINARY

A GOOD CUP OF COFFEE CAN MEAN THE WORLD TO US, literally. Taking in the aroma, taste, and body of a freshly brewed cup, pictures form in one's mind of the coffee-growing countries we have visited. We see the volcanic peaks, rich black soil, and terraced hillsides in Central America or recall the families and friendly faces of the coffee-growing communities of Costa Rica and Guatemala. An Asia/Pacific blend can transport us to the lush green rice paddies of Sulawesi or Sumatra where arabica trees thrive. We can taste the sunlight that dries the beans of Indonesia or the indigenous spices that perfume a blend. We recall the tiny cups of dark, smoky coffee ground by hand and served with reverence and reflection in Ethiopian villages. We swirl on our palates the flavors of tradition, pride, diversity, and the vastness of the African continent.

We have had the good fortune to travel the world, meet extraordinary people, and enjoy spectacular landscapes. In exchange for this great luck, we feel a tremendous responsibility to maintain the traditions of these villages and people. Personal contact is what drives us to train our partners to be true to the international history and culture of coffee. We want Starbucks customers to taste what we taste, to take a similar journey when they choose their coffee. We want them to understand the way we think of coffee, which is that "geography is a flavor."

We had this notion in mind when we first met Marcus Samuelsson. We had invited him to create a signature blend of coffee that would enhance and reflect the origins of his special style of cooking. It can be a bit intimidating to be in the company of such a culinary celebrity. Luckily, Marcus is warm, genuine, and friendly.

Our conversations and interactions were lively and educational. Marcus's ability to detect flavors and use descriptive "coffee language" was exceptional.

Marcus, of course, is a true artist, and he demonstrated a knack for coffee blending from the start. Ultimately, he decided on what we called Ubora Blend—a mixture of washed Ethiopian coffees with jasmine, citrus, and pepper essences paired with the floral flavors and cocoa notes of Rwandan beans. The finished blend typified his cuisine. Dishes that seem representative of this style are the elegant Chermoula-Roasted Bass on page 103 and the humble Black-Eyed Peas on page 85.

Marcus shares his stories of the land, the people and the traditions of a chosen country through his artfully prepared dishes. He takes diners, and now readers, on the sensory journeys to which we aspire. If "geography is a flavor," then Marcus is more than just a world traveler—he is a welcoming ambassador and a great friend.

Scott McMartin
Director of
Coffee Education

Andrew Linnemann
Master Coffee Roaster

PREFACE

FOR AS LONG AS I CAN REMEMBER, I'VE HAD AFRICA ON MY MIND. I was born Kassahun Tsegie in a small village about two hours northeast of Addis Ababa, Ethiopia, in 1970 and, like thousands of others, was placed in an orphanage three years later, when my mother died in a tuberculosis epidemic. My older sister, Fantaye, and I were among the lucky ones: a Red Cross nurse arranged for my parents, Lennart and Ann Marie Samuelsson, to adopt us. When we left for Sweden we put our Ethiopian life behind us: we were renamed Linda and Marcus and lived a typical Swedish upbringing—ice skating in the winter, playing soccer in the summer, and traveling through Europe on vacation. It was an idyllic childhood as far removed from the fate we might have met as could be imagined, and although I had no memories of Ethiopia, and Sweden was the only home I knew, always in the back of my mind I dreamed of and yearned for the day I would visit Africa again.

My mother tells me that on the day she brought Linda and me home from the airport, she woke up to find us pounding on the door of the refrigerator because after the deprivation of our life in Ethiopia, we'd seen all the food coming out of it and wanted more. We would never want for food again. Growing up, I was surrounded by food. My grandmother, who lived down the street, was constantly preparing traditional Swedish meals for us. I spent many weekends at her side, learning about food from start to finish: picking apples, making jams, hunting for mushrooms, pickling our garden harvest, and more. She passed her love of food on to me, and because of her teachings, every job I have ever had has had some connection to food: scaling fish, working at a bakery, manning a hot dog stand, selling ice cream, and finally, on the line at local restaurants. It came as no surprise to my parents when, at age sixteen, I decided to become a chef and enrolled in culinary school. After apprenticeships in Switzerland, France, and Austria, I landed in New York City for a yearlong stint at Restaurant Aquavit. Here, my curiosity about my homeland grew as the city's strong African community opened up before me: I played soccer with a group of guys from Morocco, worked with a crew of cooks and dishwashers from West Africa, ordered Senegalese takeout for dinner after a long day at the restaurant, and tasted soul food for the first time in Harlem. Most meaningfully, I tapped into the city's community of Ethiopians, visiting restaurants like Ghenet, a tranquil spot in NoLIta, and Meskerem, a restaurant around the corner from my first Manhattan apartment in Hell's Kitchen. Of all the wonders that New York held for me as a young chef, what appealed to me the most—and ultimately made me want to make New York my home—was that for the first time in my life I learned about a different side of my identity, beyond being a Swedish man. Here, I had found a place where I was welcomed as a Swede but where I could also explore my heritage as an Ethiopian, all while fitting in as a "typical" New Yorker.

In 1998, I returned to Ethiopia with my best friend, Mesfin Asefa. Like me, Mesfin is an Ethiopian raised in Sweden. Unlike me, he moved to Sweden with his parents and has an extended family in Addis Ababa that he visits once a year. On the first day of our visit, Mesfin's aunt and uncle invited us over for a traditional Ethiopian dinner that was as lavish as a Thanksgiving feast. As we sat in their kitchen scooping up chunks of spicy doro wett (traditional chicken stew) with pieces of injera, the sour, spongy, crepelike bread that is the foundation of Ethiopian cuisine, I was struck by the importance cooking and eating hold in day-to-day life in my native country. Here in this land with such a conflicted past—it's referred to as the land of milk and honey in the Bible, is the home of Rastafarian culture, and was transformed by the reign (1930–1974) of Emperor Haile Selassie, but is known to most Westerners as an area of poverty and famine—each meal is a carefully prepared feast of dishes whose recipes have been handed down through generations. The rich legacy of countless Ethiopian housewives is apparent when shopping at the lively Merkato in the heart of Addis Ababa and when feasting on the sumptuous, vividly flavored meals that families enjoy together every day of the week. Sitting down to a meal where the company is savored as much as the food has always been the cornerstone of life in Ethiopia, as it is in most African countries, and this emphasis on savoring the moment intrigued me as much as the rich and varied flavors.

I returned home filled with inspiration. As a chef, I see food as a window into a culture and I was eager to learn more about my homeland. Ethiopia's rich culture is readily apparent in its food and dining rituals. I wondered, how had other African cultures built their own unique traditions and cuisines, and what would they tell me about their histories?

To my surprise, I found that very little has been written about African cookery. It is the birthplace of mankind and the continent where fire—and cooking—were discovered. Nearly 900 million people call Africa home and 36 million Americans can trace their roots to the continent. People have been working, singing, dancing, laughing, living, and eating there for four million years. But from a food point of view, Africa is largely the undiscov-ered continent. If I wanted to learn about Africa's cuisine, I realized, I'd have to do it on my own.

In my eagerness to discover more, I pored over cookbooks like Jessica Harris's wonderful collection, dug for more books at bookstores like New York's Kitchen Arts & Letters, wandered through the galleries of the Museum for African Art in Queens, and returned to visit different parts of the continent as often as my schedule would allow. Along the way, I talked with an incredible number of generous people from all over Africa who proudly shared their favorite dishes, ingredients, techniques, traditions, and memories with me. Soon I found myself incorporating these flavors into new recipes, crafting a new approach to cooking that incorporated my newly discovered passion for this age-old continent. Out of this, the idea for **Discovery of a Continent**—a cookbook that celebrates my rediscovery of the feasts and pleasures of the continent of my birth and brings it to life for people who may have never thought about Africa from a culinary perspective—was born.

Since that first trip to Ethiopia, I've returned many times to visit new friends I've made there. But the most meaningful of all my Ethiopian experiences came on my most recent trip. I'd always thought we had been orphaned, but my sister discovered that our biological father, Tsegie, was still alive. In April 2005, I met him in that small village where I was born and where he still lives as a priest and a farmer, along with eight half brothers and sisters whom I never knew I had. Discovering this ready-made family in the Ethiopian highlands completely personalized Africa for me in a way that being born there never had, and reopened old questions of what my life might have been if that twist of fate hadn't sent me to Sweden.

Especially now that I have such a personal connection to the continent, I've noticed that whenever I pick up the newspaper and read a story about Africa, it's almost always negative: war, famine, AIDS, corruption. And it's true that a lot of bad things happen in Africa. But this is not the only Africa I know. I know an Africa that is a land of great beauty, and of beautiful people. It's a land of **ubuntu**—"I am what I am because of who we all are"—the idea that there is a universal bond of sharing that connects all people, and calls for humanity toward others. This word, which comes from the South African Zulu and Xhosa tribes and has become the foundation of the new South African government, defines a traditional African spirit that I saw connecting and unifying people throughout the continent. It's a place that assaults your senses: the colors are more vibrant; the music is more intense; the flavorings are startlingly spicy and aromatic; the heat prickles your skin; the roads are crowded with an astonishing number of cars and trucks and buses overflowing with people . . . and cows and mules and chickens. It's gritty, raw, and real, and, every minute I'm there, whether I'm shopping at the market or having a leisurely meal at a small roadside restaurant, I feel in tune with life in a way that I don't anywhere else. In Africa, you are surrounded by people everywhere you go, and the spirit of community is embracing, even in the most impoverished areas. This fun, upbeat, and interesting side of the continent is missing in the newspapers, but it's alive and well and, in my opinion, the best thing about the continent.

But to me Africa is more than just a continent bounded by a specific geography. It's a concept that has touched countries around the globe and is kept alive by the African diaspora in the Caribbean, Latin America, the United States, Europe, Australia...anyplace where Africans have moved and established new homes. Just as outside influences have affected traditional African life, the spirit of Africa has spread throughout the world. I see it everywhere I go: in the shops near my home in Harlem, the soul food of the American South, the jerk dishes of the Caribbean, the carnival of Trinidad, and the music of Brazil's Bahia—a wondrous mix of African, indigenous, and European melodies and rhythms. Throughout this book, therefore, you'll find recipes inspired by these places that are not from the continent but are **of** the continent.

As life in the United States and Europe gets faster, more convenient, and more isolating, Africa reminded me about the things that matter—friends, family, community, and the sheer enjoyment of life. It's a state of mind that I hope this book will help you tap into wherever you are. Incorporate **ubuntu** into your daily life by taking time to enjoy the process of cooking, and let your connections to other people be the centerpiece of your meals: shop and prepare food with friends and family, and linger over meals for hours. Get in touch with your food: when cooking, use a mortar and pestle instead of the mixer, or put aside the measuring cups and spoons and instead use a handful here and a pinch there. Don't just try new foods, try eating them a new way—with your hands, African-style. All this will help bring the looser, freer, more relaxed spirit of Africa into your own home.

As you use this book and discover for yourself the soul of this "new" cuisine, I hope that you, too, will come to have **ubuntu** in your heart, and Africa on your mind.

I found that very little has been written about African cookery. It is the birthplace of mankind and the continent where fire—and cooking—were discovered.

To UNDERSTAND AFRICAN COOKING, YOU HAVE TO UNDERSTAND AFRICA. But understanding this enormous continent is no easy task. People often speak about Africa as if the entire continent were one homogeneous place. Nothing could be further from the truth, for Africa is a land of contrasts, stretching from the arid deserts of the Sahara, to the lush, tropical rain forests of the Congo, to the verdant, fertile farmlands of South Africa. It is the second largest continent on the planet, covering nearly 12 million square miles, with more than fifty-five countries.

It's a land of diversity, where more than eight hundred languages and dialects are spoken and every major religion is practiced. It's also a land of turbulence, with ever-shifting borders and governments. Throughout its thousands of years of history, Africa has been explored and exploited by foreign powers, and the colonization and near constant warfare the continent has endured has left much of it impoverished, with an ever-evolving culture. The result is a continent with rich and varied societies and a distinctive array of arts, crafts, music, traditions, and celebrations, all of which make each region and country unique and special.

This uniqueness extends to the foods of the continent as well. Africa's place in history as a land of conquest has resulted in cuisines based on simple preparations that make the most of what is available. Most of the cooking is what we think of as "poor man's food": simple stews, grilled meats and fish, steamed vegetables, filling side dishes, and a range of breads. Yet these simple foods are anything but dull. African cooks coax flavor from every piece of

meat, fish, poultry, or vegetable, and no scrap is wasted. Chilies and spices are used generously to enliven dishes with an often unexpected vibrance. Ingredients range from those native to the continent—fava beans, black-eyed peas, okra, sesame seeds, yams—to the spices, limes, oranges, tomatoes, peppers, and corn introduced by explorers, traders, and settlers from Europe, the Middle East, India, and the rest of Asia.

Hospitality is a hallmark of the continent, with meals as the gathering time for friends and families. Throughout many parts of Africa, traditional meals are served around a large table, with a communal platter in the center. A jug or dish of water is passed around, so guests can wash their hands before dipping into the foods that make up a typical meal. In places such as Mali, Nigeria, Eritrea, and Somalia, fingers are used in place of knife and fork to scoop up bites of the various meats and stews, and it's considered a sign of politeness to leave a little food on the plate to indicate you've had enough to eat.

To write about Africa is to accept that in a continent so vast, you can never experience it all, or convey all the wonders it holds. I've grouped African cuisine into four geographic regions—North, West, East, and Southern—by identifying similar techniques, ingredients, and approaches that are used throughout the areas. But in truth this vastly oversimplifies the richness of the variety that can be found not just from country to country but from village to village. In this book, I focus on the countries I've seen and experienced, and so I am certain I'm omitting much of the rich and beautiful culture of the countries I have yet to explore. Following,

I give an overview of each region and the cooking styles that loosely connect the countries within each region.

NORTH AFRICA

Perhaps the Africa that's most familiar outside of the continent is the Africa of the Maghreb, the region including the countries of Morocco, Algeria, Tunisia, Sudan, and Libya. This colorful land of mystery is a place of fascination to most Westerners, and with good reason. Located just a short boat ride across the Mediterranean from Europe, it nevertheless feels like a world away, with a completely foreign vibe that is as shocking as it is exciting.

In Arabic, "Maghreb" means "where the sun sets"—a reference to the region's location as the westernmost part of the Arab world. The name is apt because Islamic culture defines the region. Mosques and mazes of medinas dominate city landscapes and no end of bizarre experiences can be found in the bazaars, where carpets, spices, teas, trinkets, and more can be found. It's a land saturated in color—the red earth tones of the desert, the jewel tones of tiled buildings, and great swathes of green landscape.

North Africa encompasses a varied climate, stretching from the tropical coastal regions, to the frigid tips of the Atlas Mountains, to the parched edges of the great Sahara. Years of French, Spanish, and German occupation left very little impact on the region. The food, with a harmonious blend of floral spices, bears little resemblance to either European or sub-Saharan African cuisine. Lamb is the dominant meat, and couscous and tagines are the immediately recognizable foods.

Although it borders the Maghreb, Egypt's culture, traditions, and food have more in common with the Middle East than with its immediate neighbors. When most people think of Egypt, romantic images of the Sphinx, pyramids, pharaohs, and mummies come to mind, but this country's modern-day life is just as intriguing as its ancient history. The streets of Cairo are alive with merchants and shoppers, and modern-day skyscrapers and condominium towers are just minutes from the majestic ancient marvels, which have been attracting tourists since the days of the ancient Greeks and Romans. The Nile River is the country's lifeline, bringing fertility to the Nile Valley and Delta as it flows from the Sudanese border to the Mediterranean Sea. It's easy to see why the ancient peoples worshipped the river and the life it gave. Although the days of paganism are long past, religion still plays a large part in day-to-day life in Egypt, where Islam, Judaism, and Christianity coexist. Pigeon, broad beans, falafel, spiced breads, and hard-boiled eggs are just a few of the foods with ancient roots in Egyptian cooking, and it's worth noting that culinarily a huge debt is owed to the ancient Egyptians, who created beer, bread, and foie gras—three things found all over the world today.

WEST AFRICA

Defining West Africa is a daunting task. This vast region, nearly as large as the continental United States, comprises seventeen countries—Mauritania, Senegal, the Gambia, Guinea, Guinea-Bissau, Sierra Leone, Liberia, Côte d'Ivoire, Mali, Burkina Faso, Ghana, Togo, Benin, Niger, Nigeria, Cameroon, and Cape Verde—that share similar geography, history, and traditions, but are still home to countless differences. Within this region, I include five more countries that are not typically categorized as West Africa geographically, but which share a common culinary bond with the region—Chad, Central African Republic, Equatorial Guinea, Gabon, and São Tomé and Principe.

Except for the very northern reaches, which occupy the southern fringes of the Sahara, most of West Africa is tropical savanna as far as the eye can see. In this sweltering climate, old-time hospitality is a given and strangers are greeted with a warm welcome and handshake. No home is entered without the offer of food and drink, and all day long women are at work preparing meals that range from small gatherings to grand feasts. These foods tend to be humble, with the emphasis on starch served with a stew or soup made with fish, chicken, or such bush meats as cane rat, gazelle, or monkey. Chilies are present in many dishes, especially in southern Nigeria, where the food is blisteringly hot.

Traveling through the region is a dizzying juxtaposition of old and new. The cities are crammed with cars, people chatting on cell phones, and every other modern convenience, while in the rural farm areas people perform tasks just as they might have hundreds of years ago. Food is still cooked outside in pots set over a three-stone fire, and meats and fish are wrapped in banana leaves and set in the ashes to steam. A common early morning scene in one of West Africa's remote villages is that of two young women with perfect posture facing each other over a giant mortar and pestle as they share the task of pounding groundnuts (what we know as peanuts) to make mafé, the famed groundnut stew of the region. Later in the day, the silhouettes of men scaling the skinny trunks of palm trees to retrieve bottles filled with fresh palm wine can be seen throughout the flat countryside.

This ancient land has a far-reaching history of tribal kingdoms and empires, but apart from Liberia, which was established in the 1840s by the United States as a home for freed slaves, today's West African countries are all former colonies of the French, British, or Portuguese. Much of the slave trade was based in West Africa; these slaves carried their culinary traditions with them, introducing native foods such as okra, black-eyed peas, sweet potatoes, watermelon, and sesame seeds to the faraway lands they were taken to.

EAST AFRICA

If you only know Africa from the movies, chances are the landscape of East Africa is what you picture. This stunningly picturesque region—encompassing Eritrea, Somalia, Djibouti, Ethiopia, Kenya, Tanzania, Uganda, Rwanda, Burundi, Congo, Malawi, and Zambia—is home to a dramatic landscape of seemingly endless savannas, the sparkling blue waters of Lake Victoria, tropical rain forests, the history-rich Red Sea, and the peaks of the mythical Mount Kilimanjaro. Lions, gazelles, zebras, ostriches, monkeys, baboons, gorillas, jackals, mongooses, hyenas, cheetahs, elephants, rhinos, warthogs, hippos, and more roam this dramatic natural wonderland, and the acres of parkland that have been set aside as preserves attract thousands of visitors on safari each year.

The Great Rift Valley that runs through much of the region is known as the cradle of humanity because human life is thought to have originated here. Perhaps it is because it is where mankind began that East Africa attracts people from all over the world, beginning at least as early as 700 A.D., when Arabs from the Arabian Peninsula and Persia settled to establish trading posts along the Indian Ocean, eventually intermarrying with native Africans to create the Swahili culture that now dominates the region. The Arabs brought their spices and cooking techniques with them, but it was later settlements by Indian traders that left the most indelible mark on the cuisine of the region, as they introduced their curries, spice blends, and breads to the foods of the region.

As in the rest of Africa, starch is the staple of the diet, stretched with a small amount of soup or stew for flavor. Ugali, a thick, bland porridge made from cornmeal or millet flour, is the most common staple and a favorite of many of the people I met. Fish and shellfish, both fresh and dried, are abundant along the coastal saltwater areas and inland lakes and rivers. Cattle are commonly considered a sign of wealth, not food, particularly by the legendary Masai herdsmen who live off the milk and blood of their herds.

Although it is geographically part of East Africa, my homeland of Ethiopia bears little resemblance to its surrounding area and deserves special mention. The only country in Africa never colonized by a foreign power, Ethiopia has a remarkably intact culture and a completely distinctive cuisine based on injera (a spongy, crepelike sourdough bread made from a grain called teff) and a variety of meat, fish, poultry, and vegetarian stews.

SOUTHERN AFRICA

Of all the places I visited in Africa, perhaps the one I most anticipated seeing was South Africa's Cape Town. My friend Jessica Harris, a noted African food historian, once referred to Cape Town as the Cape of Good Cooks because of the well-deserved reputation Cape Malay cooks have earned for their artful blending of Malaysian, Indian, European, and Afrikaner cooking. Originally brought to South Africa as slaves for the Dutch farmer colonists known as the Boers, the Cape Malays forged their own culture, creating a distinct set of traditions, customs, and foods that

soon spread into the black and Afrikaner worlds. Their beautifully balanced bredies (spiced mutton with vegetables), sosaties (spiced mutton or lamb skewers with apricots), koesisters (spiced dough-nuts), and other wonderful dishes dazzled, delighted, and inspired me.

But Southern Africa is more than just Cape Malay culture. Homo sapiens have been rang-ing the stunning landscapes of South Africa, Botswana, Zimbabwe, Lesotho, Swaziland, and Namibia for more than fifty thousand years, and the many tribes of the region have developed their own distinctive cultures. It is one of the most beautiful areas of the world, featuring the best of what Africa has to offer—generous natural resources, sparkling gems, the awe-inspiring Victoria Falls, the vast Kalahari Desert, enormous game parks, stunning cities, turquoise waters, and ancient ruins that date back to the earliest days of man.

Beyond the coast, Southern Africa's island nations offer a different perspective, with a glo-rious fusion of influences from around the world combined in a uniquely African way. There's no other country like Madagascar, the fourth largest island on Earth—its emerald forests and shimmering streams are home to animals and plants found nowhere else on the planet, includ-ing rare lemurs, birds, and frogs that attract vis-itors from around the world. Culinarily, Madagascar is on the map for the fine vanilla and coffee that Malagasy farmers produce. The breathtaking landscape of Comoros, an island nation off the coast of Madagascar, ranges from steep mountains to low hills, while the more politically stable islands of Seychelles and Mauritius attract tourists with their friendly peo-ple, azure waters, and white beaches.

To the north, Angola and Mozambique, on opposite coasts of the continent, were once sis-ter colonies of Portugal and to this day maintain a distinct similarity in their culture and in their food. Portuguese traders introduced corn, beans, chili peppers, and more from their colonies in the New World, and these foods were swiftly incorporated into the native diet.

W HEN I BEGAN TRAVELING THROUGH THIS INCREDIBLY DIVERSE LAND, I went with preconceptions about the food I would find. But Africa never stopped surprising me and by the time I left, those preconceptions had all broken down. The continent is so huge and home to so many people from all over the world that there are no "rules"—as soon as you think "no one does this here," you'll find someone who does. It made writing about the foods of the entire continent a challenge.

As I was working on this project, a number of people said to me, "Africa is so huge and so diverse. How can you possibly write a cookbook about the whole continent?" I understand their question, and from the start had a clear idea that this book would not be a definitive encyclopedia of African cooking. Rather, this cookbook is a reflection of the Africa I've seen, experienced, and appreciated. It's a very personal voyage that highlights my own interpretation of Africa and its cuisines, and it provides just an overview of the foods of this vast area, giving you a taste of what the continent has to offer. I feature traditional recipes for dishes that have been handed down through generations, but I've also created my own interpretations of dishes that take the African tastes and techniques I've grown to love as a jumping-off point to create my own African-inspired cuisine, just as other chefs over the last twenty or thirty years have introduced the wonderful flavors of Italian, Asian, and Latin cooking. As more and more people travel to the continent and African ingredients become increasingly available, it's a cuisine whose time has come, and my goal with this book is to help you bring your own dream of Africa into your home kitchen.

DISCOVERY OF A CONTINENT

INGREDIENTS

PANTRY

The African kitchen is not as foreign as you may expect—many of the ingredients used in every-day cooking are found in pantries around the world. There are a number of ingredients, how-ever, that either are unique to Africa or are used in ways that you may not be accustomed to.

Banana Leaves: The wide, striated leaves of the banana tree are frequently used in West Africa to wrap foods for steaming. The leaves are very long, measuring 3 to 4 feet, and should be cut to the needed size. They can be found in Latin, Asian, Caribbean, and African grocery stores and are usually sold frozen.

Beans: Beans are a common source of protein throughout Africa, particularly in countries like Ethiopia, where a large number of religious fast days are observed. I prefer cooking with dried beans rather than using canned beans, which often have a metallic taste. Cover dried beans with cold water and soak for at least 8 hours, or overnight, before cooking them.

Brown Sugar: Brown sugar is manufactured throughout the African continent. My favorite is an organic fair-trade raw-cane demerara from Malawi, which is sold under the Wholesome Sweetners brand at many upscale grocery stores. It has an intense, multifaceted flavor that really stands out in a recipe.

Bulgur: Arab traders introduced many foods to North Africa, including bulgur, a type of cracked wheat. This highly nutritious grain can be found in larger supermarkets, health food stores, and specialty stores, as well as through online sources.

Cardamom: Tanzania is one of the world's largest growers of cardamom, a lovely aromatic spice used to flavor soups, stews, baked goods, and, in Arabic countries, coffee. I suggest buy-ing whole cardamom and grinding it yourself rather than buying preground, as the flavor is much more intense. This is true of all spices, but the flavor difference is especially noticeable for this spice. White and green cardamom pods are available; I prefer white cardamom, which has been bleached, because I think it gives a cleaner, truer taste. Avoid brown or black cardamom, also known as false cardamom, which comes from a different plant. And use cardamom sparingly, as the intense flavor goes a long way.

Cassava: Originally from South America, cassa-va was brought to Africa by Spanish and Portuguese traders and quickly became a staple food. Probably the most well-known use of the cigar-shaped root is in West Africa, where it is cooked and pounded into a mash called fufu. In addition, the leaves are used as a green veg-etable, while the roots are also dried to make cassava meal and tapioca. There are two main types of cassava, bitter and sweet. Cyanide compounds occur naturally in the bitter variety, making it poisonous unless cooked, so only the sweet variety is approved by the USDA for sale in the United States; to be on the safe side, I suggest rinsing any cassava thoroughly before preparing it. Cassava, also known as manioc or yuca, is available in African and Hispanic markets. Look for roots that are firm and even in color and texture.

Chickpeas: Chickpeas were first cultivated by the ancient Egyptians, and they have played an important part in African cooking ever since. They are pureed into a vegetarian paste for hummus, crushed and fried to make falafel, or stirred whole into stews or couscous. I prefer dried chickpeas, which need to be soaked in cold water for at least 8 hours before using, to canned. Look for whole, uniformly colored beans with no cracks.

Chilies: Heat is one of the hallmarks of African cooking, especially in West Africa, Mozambique, Angola, Tunisia, and the Horn region, where a blisteringly hot dose of chili peppers is added to many dishes. Chilies originated in Mexico and were brought to Africa by Spanish and Portuguese traders in the 1500s. The variety of chilies available today is astonishing. For the recipes in this book, I use the more readily available serrano, jalapeño, bird's-eye, and Scotch bonnet, but feel free to experiment with any different varieties you may find, varying the amount you use according to your personal heat preference. Most of the heat in chilies comes from capsaicin, a chemical found in the seeds and ribs. It is very potent and can burn the skin or your eyes if you rub them after handling, so be careful not to touch your face, and thoroughly wash your hands afterward.

Chocolate: Chocolate is as popular in Africa as it is elsewhere in the world. Use a high-quality brand like Scharffen Berger, Valrhona, or Callebaut, all of which are made with the choicest cacao beans for a wonderful flavor profile.

Cinnamon: A familiar flavor around the world, cinnamon has earned a place of importance in the African kitchen, used in the tagines of Morocco, the Indian-inspired stews of the eastern coast, and the Malay dishes of Cape Town, among others. There are two types of cinnamon. Cassia is the most common in the United States, but I prefer Ceylon, or true cinnamon, which has a milder, sweeter, more refined flavor. When possible, buy whole sticks instead of ground cinnamon, which is usually the cassia variety.

Clarified Butter: Clarified butter is the basis of nit'ir qibe, the spiced butter used in almost all of Ethiopia's stews. Because all the milk solids have been removed, clarified butter can be cooked over high temperatures without burning and can be stored for much longer without going rancid, an important point for cooks living in Ethiopia's scorching climate. To make clarified butter, heat at least ½ pound of butter in a saucepan over medium-low heat, without stirring, until the milk fats separate and fall to the bottom of the pan. Carefully skim the foam from the top, then pour the golden liquid butter into a container, leaving the milk solids in the pan. Tightly covered, clarified butter will keep for up to a month in the refrigerator.

Coconut Milk: Coconuts are used throughout the world's tropical areas, and both the milk and meat are common ingredients in many African recipes. Fresh coconut milk is made by combining equal parts hot water and coconut meat and blending the mixture in a blender or food processor, then straining the resulting mash through a cheesecloth. Canned coconut milk, readily available in most grocery stores, can be used in any recipe calling for coconut milk; just be sure to shake the can vigorously before opening, as it separates upon standing.

Coffee: My birthplace of Ethiopia is also the birthplace of coffee. Wild Arabica coffee beans originated in the forest of the Kaffa region, where, according to legend, a local goatherd named Kaldi noticed his goats frolicking energetically after chewing on the berries and decided to try them himself. To this day, coffee still grows in the wild throughout Ethiopia, and its production is a vital part of the country's economy. The Sidamo region produces one of my favorite coffees, a full, earthy blend with great texture. Coffee production is not limited to Ethiopia. Neighbor countries Kenya and Tanzania grow some of the best coffees available in the world.

Couscous: When it comes to North African cooking, no other food compares in importance to couscous. Called **seksu** in Berber, this pasta is still formed by hand into tiny balls, then steamed in a perforated pot known as a **couscoussier** throughout all of North Africa. Although semolina flour is the grain most commonly used as the base for the couscous sold in North America, throughout North Africa it can be made with any variety of grains, including barley, unripened wheat, or wheat bran. A form of couscous made of millet flour is found in western Africa, particularly in Mali.

Ginger: Ginger is used both medicinally and culinarily throughout Africa. This knobby tropical rhizome lends a fresh, spicy zing to stews, soups, and beverages all over the continent. Look for firm, evenly colored ginger with smooth skin. Peel away the tough skin before using. Store, tightly wrapped, in the refrigerator for up to 3 weeks.

Lemongrass: The sour, lemony flavor and fragrance of lemongrass is most associated with the cooking of Southeast Asia, but it is an important component of African cooking, too, especially along the eastern coast, where the Asian influences are the strongest. African cooks use the whole stalk, chopping and crushing the root end to flavor meat and fish dishes and infusing the top part in water to make a deliciously refreshing tea.

Lentils: Lentils are popular all over the African continent, particularly along the Indian-influenced eastern coast; the Horn region of Ethiopia, Eritrea, and Somalia; and Egypt. Hearty and filling, they make wonderful vegetarian stews. Brown lentils can be found at most supermarkets; red and yellow lentils are available at Middle Eastern and Indian markets, as well as many health food stores and supermarkets.

Mango: In recent years, the mango has become widely available throughout the United States and it's not hard to see why it's so popular: this beautiful golden-fleshed fruit has a heady fragrance and bursts with sweet juices. Choose mangoes that give just slightly when squeezed; if only unripened mangoes are available, place them in a paper bag to speed up the ripening process. Following the Indian tradition, in Africa green mangoes are used like a vegetable in salads and savory side dishes. Green mangoes can be found at Caribbean, Asian, and Indian markets. Mango pits are very large; to pit the fruit, use a sharp knife to cut the flesh away from the pit.

Merguez Sausage: Bright red merguez sausages from Tunisia, Algeria, and Morocco are made from beef or lamb, rather than pork, in keeping with Islamic dietary laws. They get their spiciness from fiery harissa. These small sausages are typically grilled or fried or cut into pieces and stirred into couscous dishes. You can find them at ethnic markets and some specialty butchers.

Okra: I had always thought of okra as a vegetable of the American South, so it came as a surprise to learn that it originated in my native Ethiopia and is used throughout Africa. It is used to thicken soups and stews, and it is the prime ingredient in the gumbos of the American South. Okra is available frozen or canned, but when possible I suggest using fresh, which you can find at specialty markets and some grocery stores. When buying fresh okra, look for firm, bright green pods.

Papaya: This delicately scented fruit is used in both ripe and unripened form by African cooks. When ripe, it is typically eaten as a snack or a sweet ending to a meal; unripened, it is commonly used like a vegetable in salads and savory side dishes. Like many other foods that are now common in the continent, the papaya was brought to Africa by Spanish and Portuguese traders from their Central and South American colonies. When purchasing ripe papayas, look for fruit with golden-yellow skin that gives just slightly when squeezed. Green papayas are firm with a solid green skin.

Peanuts: Though it may seem as American as baseball and apple pie, the peanut (or groundnut, as it is known throughout Africa) is believed to have originated in South America and been introduced to East and West Africa by Portuguese traders in the sixteenth century. Today, peanuts are commonly used in stews and soups across Africa, and peanut oil is used for frying. Peanuts are usually sold roasted. For the recipes in this book, you can use salted dry-roasted peanuts, but if you want to buy them unshelled, look for clean, intact shells. In some recipes I call for blanched peanuts, which give a moister, meatier flavor to the finished dish.

Plantains: Plantains are eaten throughout sub-Saharan Africa and in regions around the world where African slaves carried their culinary traditions, including the Caribbean and Brazil. Unlike their cousin the banana, plantains are eaten both ripe and unripe. Unripened green plantains are typically used in savory dishes, while ripe yellow plantains are used for sweet preparations. In recipes that call for plantains, I've indicated whether to use the green or yellow fruit. Yellow plantains can be peeled as easily as a banana, but the skins of green plantains are thick and tough and cling to the fruit, often breaking off in little pieces when you try to peel it. The easiest way to peel a green plantain is to cut off both ends, then make four evenly spaced incisions with a sharp knife down the length of the fruit. Pull off the sections crosswise rather than lengthwise for a perfectly peeled plantain.

Rice: Rice is one of Africa's most important foods and is eaten throughout most of the continent, from the Malay culture of South Africa, to the Indian-influenced eastern coast, to the Arab-style dishes of Morocco, Algeria, Tunisia, and Egypt. Rice is particularly important in parts of western Africa, including Senegal, where short-grain rice is an integral part of national dishes like chep-bu-jen and jollof rice. In fact, it was slaves from West Africa who brought their knowledge of rice cultivation to the Carolinas, where rice farming thrived for more than three centuries. Broken jasmine rice from Asia, which I find at many of the African markets near my home in Harlem, can be used as a short-grain rice.

Sumac: Sumac comes from the berries of a type of sumac bush, which are dried and usually sold ground. It adds a sour, acidic note to many Middle Eastern and North African dishes. Most notably, it is one of the principal ingredients in za'atar, the popular spice blend. You can find sumac in ethnic grocery stores and through online sources.

Tamarind: This sour tropical fruit—known for its use in Indian curries and chutneys and in Worcestershire sauce—is also a popular ingredient in northern and eastern Africa, as well as in the African diaspora in the Caribbean. The fruit, also called Indian date or tamarindo, grows in knobby, brittle pods that contain a sticky brown pulp and numerous seeds. You can find tamarind at Indian and Indonesian markets, as a paste in cans, as concentrated pulp in jars, or dried into bricks. To make your own tamarind paste, pour ½ cup boiling water over 2 tablespoons dried tamarind, let the mixture sit for a few minutes, and then stir with a fork to make a thick, dark paste. If dried tamarind is unavailable, you can make a reasonably similar substitute by combining ¼ cup each of chopped dried dates, chopped dried apricots, and fresh lemon juice in a food processor and pulsing until smooth; tightly covered, this will keep in the refrigerator for up to a month.

Tapioca: Most Americans are familiar with tapioca pudding and its small pearl-shaped pellets. Tapioca is made from dried cassava, one of the staples of the African kitchen. Pearl tapioca is found in any supermarket; tapioca flour is available in many Asian markets and health food stores. See **Cassava** on page 1.

Teff: This nutty, nutrient-dense grain grows in the highlands of Ethiopia and is the basis for injera, the bread served at nearly all Ethiopian meals. Once nearly impossible to find in the United States, it is becoming available in organic and health food markets, primarily thanks to farmers in Idaho who have recently begun cultivating it; it is also available from online sources.

Vanilla Bean: The humble-looking vanilla bean is loaded with flavor that is anything but unassuming. The best vanilla beans come from Madagascar, Tahiti, and Mexico. Unripened vanilla beans, which I saw growing at a spice farm in Zanzibar, are green and flavorless, but after being cured in the sun for months, they explode with familiar vanilla flavor. To use, split the bean lengthwise with a sharp knife and scrape out the seeds. Then use just the seeds, or both the seeds and the pod, depending on the recipe. I often put the scraped pod in the sugar canister for a week or so to infuse the sugar with a light vanilla flavor. You can find vanilla beans at larger supermarkets, in gourmet stores, and via the Internet.

Yam: Yams have been cultivated in Africa for more than ten thousand years. They are one of the staple foods of the continent, particularly in West Africa, where numerous feast days celebrate the nutritious tuber. In fact, I learned that in Guinea the word for "yam" is the same as the word for "eat." Here in the United States, sweet potatoes are often mislabeled as yams; true yams are not widely available, though you can sometimes find them at ethnic markets and specialty stores. If you can't find true yams, substitute an equal amount of sweet potatoes.

AT FIRST GLANCE, AFRICAN FOOD SEEMS VERY STRAIGHTFORWARD—meats grilled over an open flame, slow-cooked stews stretched with vegetables and offal, and bland, starchy sides that fill the belly for a full day's work. But my travels throughout the continent put an end to this assumption—as I ate my way through Africa, in country after country I found the cooking to be startlingly flavorful and full of surprises.

You can't begin to think about African cooking without first understanding the importance of spice blends, which are used to elevate simple cooking techniques to an excitingly varied and intensive level. Just as European cooking relies on salt to give dimension to dishes, cooks throughout Africa use spice blends and rubs to season their meats, poultry, fish, and other seafood before and after cooking. With blends that vary from region to region—ranging from sweet to spicy with varying degrees of heat, and featuring everything from hot chili peppers or peppermint leaves to sesame seeds and ginger—it's an exciting and flavor-packed way to eat that awed me at first bite.

In this chapter, I've compiled my favorite blends, representing the best of each region. And don't forget that these blends provide an easy way to introduce the flavors of Africa to your everyday cooking. If you don't have the time or inclination to make one of the recipes from this book but want to add a taste of Africa to your meal, just use the blend of your choice—for instance, rubbing delicately flavored ras al-hanout over a chicken breast or fiery piri piri sauce on a bass fillet next time you fire up the grill.

BERBERE

n Ethiopia, the preparation of berbere takes days—chilies are dried in the sun for three days, then ground in a mortar and pestle, mixed with ground spices, and set in the sun to dry again—and it is usually made in huge amounts.

Each Ethiopian family has its own recipe for this universal seasoning, with varying degrees of heat and spiciness. Traditionally, berbere is used to flavor Ethiopian stews, but I also like to use it as a rub for beef and lamb.

1 teaspoon fenugreek seeds

½ cup ground dried serrano chilies or other ground dried chilies

½ cup paprika

2 tablespoons salt

2 teaspoons ground ginger

2 teaspoons onion powder

1 teaspoon ground cardamom, preferably freshly ground

1 teaspoon ground nutmeg

½ teaspoon garlic powder

¼ teaspoon ground cloves

¼ teaspoon ground cinnamon

¼ teaspoon ground allspice

Finely grind the fenugreek seeds with a mortar and pestle or in an electric spice or coffee grinder. Stir together with the remaining ingredients in a small bowl until well combined.

Store in an airtight container in the refrigerator for up to 3 months.

MAKES 1 CUP

BLACK OLIVE OIL

When considering the cooking of the Mediterranean, many people look only to the north and completely overlook the countries that border the southern side of the sea. But in fact, North African cooking—especially in Morocco and Tunisia—shares many similarities with the culinary traditions of Spain, Italy, and Greece, particularly the reliance on olives, which are served at the start of every meal, and olive oils. This black olive oil is inspired by the cooking of North Africa and is great to use as a rub for lamb or fish, or even as a dressing for salad.

½ cup black olives, pitted

2 anchovy fillets, minced, or 1½ teaspoons anchovy paste

2 cups extra virgin olive oil

2 garlic cloves

2 thyme sprigs, leaves only, chopped

Combine all the ingredients in a blender and puree until smooth.

Store tightly covered in the refrigerator for up to 1 week.

MAKES 2½ CUPS

CHERMOULA

I think chermoula is a perfect representation of the best of North African culinary traditions—it's rich and varied in flavor, with underlying spiciness so you can really taste all the distinct spices. Cooks all over northern Africa use chermoula, particularly in Morocco and Tunisia, where it is typically used as a rub for fish. I like to toss it with chicken or meat when I'm grilling to add a bright and lively note of herbs and citrus with just a hint of heat.

8 garlic cloves

½ cup small parsley sprigs

⅓ cup small cilantro sprigs

Grated zest of 2 lemons

4 teaspoons paprika

2 teaspoons chili powder

2 teaspoons ground cumin

1 cup olive oil

Combine the garlic, parsley, cilantro, lemon zest, paprika, chili powder, and cumin in a blender and blend on low speed to a coarse puree; don't process until smooth. With the blender running, add the oil in a thin, steady stream and blend until a thick paste forms.

Store in a tightly covered container in the refrigerator for up to 2 weeks.

MAKES 1½ CUPS

DUQQA

The word "duqqa" is derived from the Arabic word meaning "to pound," and with good reason, because the nuts and spices are crushed together with a mortar and pestle for a richly textured result. Originally developed in the Middle East, this lovely spice blend has made its way throughout northern Africa. It's especially popular in Egypt, where it is eaten with bread dipped in olive oil at breakfast or as a snack. Recipes for duqqa vary from family to family, with mint as the signature flavor. While you can find prepared duqqa in some Middle Eastern markets, it's so easy to make and the fresh preparation is so superior in flavor and aroma that I recommend only using homemade. Do not try making this in a blender, as the sesame seeds will turn to a paste.

2 tablespoons hulled pumpkin seeds
2 tablespoons peanuts
1 teaspoon black peppercorns
2 teaspoons sesame seeds
8 mint leaves
4 thyme sprigs, leaves only
1 teaspoon coriander seeds
1 teaspoon cumin seeds
1½ teaspoons salt

Heat a small sauté pan over medium heat. Add the pumpkin seeds, peanuts, and peppercorns and toast, stirring, until fragrant, about 5 minutes. Add the sesame seeds, mint leaves, thyme leaves, coriander, and cumin and toast, stirring frequently, until fragrant, about 5 minutes.

Transfer to a mortar and grind with the pestle, or grind in an electric spice or coffee grinder until the seeds and nuts are coarsely crushed. Add the salt.

Store in a tightly covered container in the refrigerator for up to 10 days.

MAKES ½ CUP

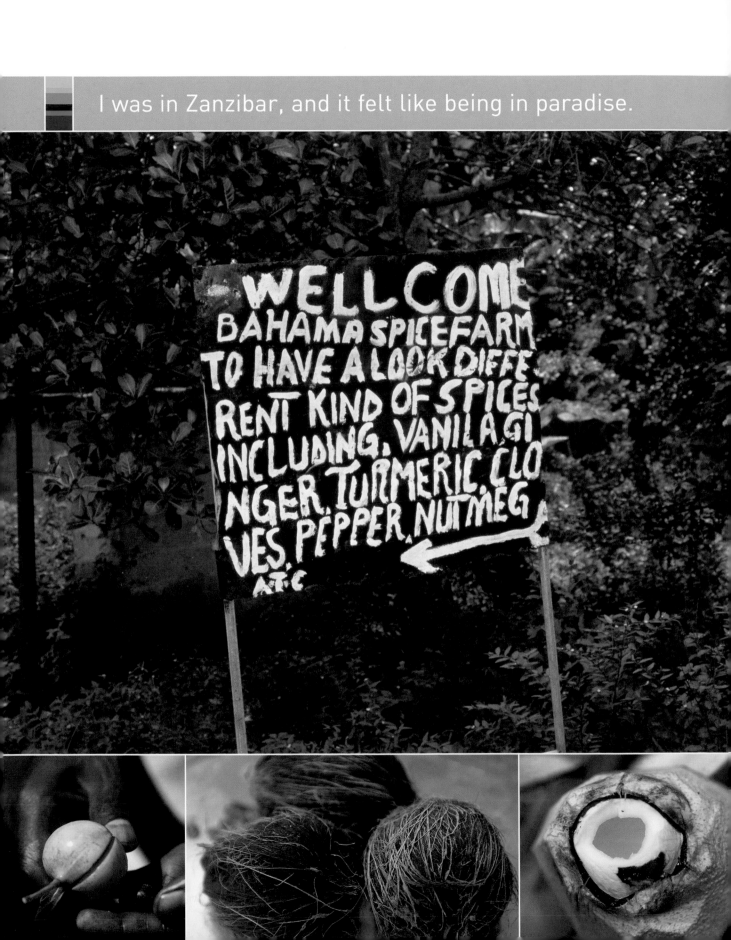

I WAS VISITING THE BAHAMA SPICE FARM, a small, private farm where the faint, musky smell of cloves and cardamom danced on the breeze. Before me stretched a riotous tangle of greenery, sprouting spices I never imagined I'd have the opportunity to see growing—much less all in one place. As a chef, seeing how the spices I use daily are cultivated was like being in my own personal garden of Eden.

A guide walked me through the farm, challenging me to recognize the different spices that grew before us. Handing me a leaf from a large tree, he urged me to smell it to see if I could recognize the aroma. I sniffed and ventured a guess—"Cinnamon?"—and he smiled, happy to have stumped me. "No, it's nutmeg," he said, cracking open the mottled yellow fruit to reveal the tough brown kernel of nutmeg at its center.

And so it went on our journey along the rambling path that ran through the spice patches. Before me, vanilla beans, ginger, cardamom, cloves, lemongrass, cocoa, cinnamon—all the magical flavors that inspire me every day—sprang from the ground, seemingly at random: a nutmeg tree here, a vanilla-bean vine there, a cinnamon tree in the distance.

At the end of the tour, one of the boys accompanying us twisted a length of rope into a figure 8, hooked his feet into it, and used it to help him shimmy up the trunk of a tall, graceful coconut tree, disappearing into the sky to send a storm of coconuts raining down on us. Back on the ground, he cracked open a coconut and handed it to me. As I sipped the fresh, warm juice, I remembered hearing that long-ago sailors passing Zanzibar used to claim they could smell the scent of cloves drifting from the island far out to sea. Today, Zanzibari farmers still eke out a living growing spices on small plots of land, but there was a time when spice plantations brought great riches to Zanzibar, a time whose legacy can still be seen in Stone Town, the faded but opulent heart of this vibrant island.

Stone Town is one of the most magical cities I've ever visited. It's a city of surprises. This exotic, mysteri-ous town is the place where the African, Arab, and Indian worlds meet. Hundreds of years ago, African fishermen, Arab and Persian traders, and Indian merchants all settled on the island. The Portuguese occupied Zanzibar beginning in 1503, but were forced out by the Omani Arabs in the late 1600s. Their defeat was followed by more than two hundred years of rule by Arab sultans.

The sultans transformed Zanzibar, introducing cloves from Madagascar and building the first spice plantations. Thanks to the spice trade, the island quickly grew rich and the newly wealthy townspeople began rebuilding their mud homes with stone. The traditional Islamic modesty of these homes was accented with beautifully carved and studded doors, which are now one of the hallmarks of Stone Town. I was told these doors served a dual purpose—their ornate carving was a way for wealthy homeowners to show off their riches, while the studs were a symbol of protection for the inhabitants.

But, as in many of the places I visited in Africa, you can't ignore history. All this grandeur has a dark side: at the height of the slave trade, as many as sixty thousand slaves a year were transported from the mainland to Zanzibar and sold to owners in Arabia, India, and French Indian Ocean possessions. I visited one of the prisons where the slaves were held—a cramped, dark, stark contrast to the stunning palaces built by the sultans who grew rich from the sale of slaves and spices.

During my brief visit, I drank in the sights, smells, and sounds of Zanzibar: fishermen sailing off in elegant dhows as the sun set over the Indian Ocean, the scent of grilled fish wafting from Stone Town's nightly waterfront market at Forodhani Gardens, and the calling of the muezzin—the crier who summons the Muslim faithful to prayer five times a day—from the mosque near our hotel. It's a place of magic and mystique, whose very name conjures up a sense of enchantment and the smell of spices.

GINGER PASTE

Ginger made its way to Africa through Middle Eastern and Asian traders and is now used throughout the continent both as a flavoring and for medicinal purposes. Use this paste to lend ginger's wonderfully distinctive pungent, peppery flavor to fish, meat, or poultry.

3 garlic cloves, minced
1 tablespoon ground ginger
1 teaspoon ground coriander
½ teaspoon chili powder
½ teaspoon ground turmeric
2 tablespoons coarsely chopped dry-roasted peanuts
1 tablespoon peanut oil
¼ cup fresh lemon juice
½ teaspoon salt
One 4-inch piece ginger, peeled and grated

Heat a small sauté pan over medium heat. Add the garlic, ground ginger, coriander, chili powder, turmeric, and peanuts and toast, stirring, until fragrant, about 2 minutes.

Transfer to a food processor. Add the oil and lemon juice and process until well combined but not smooth. Add the salt and process to blend. Before using, fold in the grated ginger.

Store in an airtight container in the refrigerator for up to 3 days.

MAKES ABOUT ½ CUP

GREEN MASALA

Masala—which is said to stem from the Arabic word for "necessities"—truly is a necessity in East African cooking. Indian traders, as well as British colonialists who had acquired a fondness for this traditional blend of chilies and spices, brought masala with them when they settled on African shores, and it is now used throughout the region. There's no one right way to make a masala—recipes vary from region to region and family to family—but I like this distinctive version, which adds a strong, balanced flavor to meat, fish, and vegetable stews. You can use it in any recipe that calls for dried curry powder.

½ cup plus 2 tablespoons olive oil
One 3-inch piece ginger, peeled and grated
4 garlic cloves, minced
8 jalapeño chilies, seeds and ribs removed, chopped
1 teaspoon cardamom seeds
1 teaspoon ground turmeric
1 teaspoon coriander seeds
2 tablespoons white wine vinegar

Heat 2 tablespoons of the olive oil in a medium sauté pan over medium heat. Add the ginger, garlic, and jalapeños and sauté until the garlic is golden, about 4 minutes. Add the cardamom, turmeric, and coriander and sauté until fragrant, about 1 minute. Remove from the heat.

Transfer to a blender, add the white wine vinegar, and blend well to combine. With the blender running on low speed, add the remaining ½ cup oil in a thin, steady stream, blending until well combined.

Store in an airtight container in the refrigerator for up to 1 week or in the freezer for up to 3 weeks.

MAKES 1 CUP

HARISSA

Typical North African flavors don't feature the spiciness you see throughout the rest of the continent. The exception is harissa, a fiery red paste that can be found in virtually every Tunisian kitchen. It's the hottest spice mix in the region—much sharper than the more floral blends typical of North African cooking—and it is usually served as an accompaniment to couscous or as a flavoring for soups and stews. When making harissa, it is preferable to freshly grind the spices for the strongest flavor.

¾ cup olive oil
2 garlic cloves, minced
1 teaspoon ground caraway
1 cup mild chili powder
1 tablespoon ground coriander
1 teaspoon salt
2 tablespoons chopped mint

Heat the oil in a small sauté pan over medium heat. When the oil shimmers, add the garlic and sauté until golden, about 4 minutes.

Remove the pan from the heat. Add the caraway, chili powder, coriander, salt, and mint and stir to combine. Let cool.

Store in an airtight container in the refrigerator for up to 2 weeks.

MAKES 1¼ CUPS

JERK MIX

Featuring notes of cinnamon, thyme, and ginger, this Jamaican-inspired rub is an excellent seasoning for chicken, pork, beef, shrimp, or firm white fish. Most Jamaican chefs grind the spices by hand in a mortar and pestle, a technique I recommend to retain the spices' natural, aromatic oils. I also suggest toasting the spices first, which enhances and mellows their flavor. If you have only ground spices on hand, it's perfectly fine to use them, but the flavors won't be as intense.

2 tablespoons olive oil

6 garlic cloves, minced

2 jalapeño chilies, seeds and ribs removed, finely chopped

1 tablespoon ground allspice

1 teaspoon ground cinnamon

1 teaspoon cayenne pepper

2 tablespoons brown sugar

1 teaspoon white pepper

1 tablespoon dried thyme

1 teaspoon salt

1 teaspoon ground ginger

4 scallions, trimmed and chopped

⅓ cup fresh lime juice

½ cup red wine vinegar

Heat the oil in a small sauté pan over medium heat. When the oil shimmers, add the garlic and jalapeños and sauté until the garlic just starts to color, about 3 minutes. Add the allspice, cinnamon, cayenne, and brown sugar and cook, stirring constantly, until the sugar melts and the mixture starts to clump together. Remove from the heat and let cool slightly.

Transfer the mixture to a blender. Add the white pepper, thyme, salt, ginger, scallions, lime juice, and red wine vinegar and blend until smooth.

Store in an airtight container in the refrigerator for up to 10 days.

MAKES 1 CUP

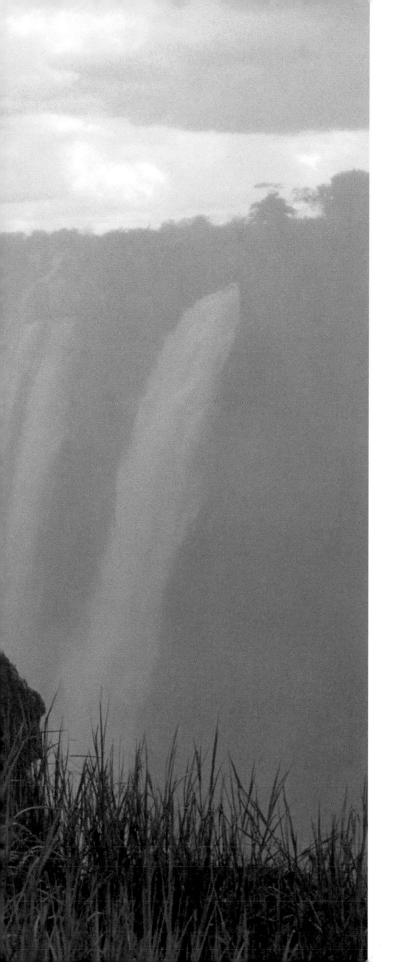

RAS AL-HANOUT

The Bedouin Arabs who settled the Maghreb in the seventh century forever changed North African cooking with their introduction of saffron, nutmeg, cinnamon, ginger, cloves, cumin, and other rich spices of the East, establishing the region as the heart of the spice trade between Europe, Africa, and the Middle East. The name "ras al-hanout" literally translates as "best of the shop." This recipe is a simple, basic spice mix that also makes an excellent rub for almost anything—chicken, lamb, or meaty fish steaks like salmon and tuna. For best results, use whole spices and grind them by hand in a mortar and pestle or spice grinder.

¼ cup ground cinnamon

2 tablespoons ground turmeric

1 tablespoon freshly ground black pepper

1½ teaspoons ground nutmeg

1½ teaspoons ground cardamom, preferably freshly ground

1½ teaspoons ground cloves

Combine all the spices in a small bowl and blend well. To intensify the flavors, lightly toast the amount you need just before using.

Store in a tightly sealed container in a cool, dark place for up to 3 weeks.

MAKES ABOUT ½ CUP

SPICED BUTTER

The spiced mixture known as nit'ir qibe, which begins with clarified butter, is kept handy in most Ethiopian kitchens to add flavor to meat and vegetable stews. In fact, virtually no meal in Ethiopia is made without nit'ir qibe, which gives the cooking its beautifully layered signature flavors. It also has a much longer shelf life than regular butter—an important consideration in poor man's cooking, where waste is not an option. The butter will solidify when chilled, but it will become liquid again when left at room temperature.

1 pound unsalted butter

½ medium red onion, coarsely chopped

1 garlic clove, minced

One 3-inch piece ginger, peeled and finely chopped

1 teaspoon fenugreek seeds

1 teaspoon ground cumin

1 teaspoon cardamom seeds

1 teaspoon dried oregano

½ teaspoon ground turmeric

8 basil leaves

Melt the butter in a medium saucepan over low heat, stirring frequently. As foam rises to the top, skim and discard it. Continue cooking, without letting the butter brown, until no more foam appears. Add the onion, garlic, ginger, fenugreek, cumin, cardamom, oregano, turmeric, and basil and continue cooking for 15 minutes, stirring occasionally.

Remove from the heat and let stand until the spices settle. Strain through a fine-mesh sieve before using.

Store in the refrigerator in a tightly covered container for up to 3 weeks.

MAKES 1½ CUPS

DISCOVERY OF A CONTINENT

ZA'ATAR

Za'atar is one of my favorites of North Africa's many spice blends. Delicate and fragrant, it has a distinctive citrusy flavor from the sumac and a rich texture that makes it an excellent rub for fish, poultry, or meats, or to add bright flavor to soups and stews. I also like to mix three parts za'atar with one part olive oil for a delicious dip for bread.

2 tablespoons sesame seeds
1 tablespoon dried thyme
1 tablespoon dried oregano
2 tablespoons ground sumac (see page 5)
1 teaspoon salt

Toast the sesame seeds in a small sauté pan over low heat until golden brown, about 1½ minutes. Remove from the heat and set aside to cool.

Mix together the thyme, oregano, and sumac in a small bowl, then stir in the sesame seeds and salt.

Store in a tightly sealed container in a cool, dark place for up to 2 weeks.

MAKES ⅓ CUP

I'VE ALWAYS THOUGHT that one of the most telling and interesting ways to learn about a country's cuisine is through its accompaniments—the condiments, relishes, toppings, and spreads that dress up local food. They can also give you a little surprise and help clue you in to a region's history. When I had my first Cape Malay meal in South Africa, the vividly spiced sambals that accompanied my meal were so reminiscent of the flavors of Indonesia and Malaysia that it was no surprise to learn that slaves from that region were brought to the Cape three centuries ago and quickly made their mark on the stodgy Dutch fare of their owners. Likewise, seeing chutneys on the tables of Tanzania immediately let me know that Indian traders and settlers had moved up and down the eastern coast, swirling together the techniques and flavors of the Indian mainland with the ingredients native to these African shores.

As far as my research went, it doesn't hurt that condiments are one of my favorite parts of eating, adding a dash of flavor and a daub of freshness to any meal. There's something so refreshing about condiments, whether it's the silken and delicate preserved lemons of Morocco—a variation of which is represented here in the Preserved Citrus Peel—or the all-American Barbeque Sauce infused with berbere and coffee, two quintessential Ethiopian ingredients.

Most of the recipes featured in this chapter will keep for at least a week, so you can build up an incredible pantry of flavorings that can be served together to create an interesting everyday meal. Try the Papaya Ketchup with a simple grilled chicken breast, spoon the Mango Sambal over a tuna steak, or set out the White Bean Puree with a baguette and some Brie the next time you want to add a little excitement to an easy weekday meal.

CONDIMENTS, SAUCES, AND DIPS

CHICKPEA-EGGPLANT DIP

Hummus is now so ubiquitous that it's hard to remember it was once an "exotic" food. It was the first Moroccan food I ever had, and since that first bite I've grown to love the simplicity of Morocco's many dips because they're so easy to enjoy. You can serve this hummus-style dip on its own with warm pita wedges, as a spread on sandwiches, or as a distinctive accompaniment to grilled fish or chicken.

2 cups dried chickpeas, soaked in cold water for 8 hours and drained

1 carrot, peeled and cut in half

1 medium Spanish onion, cut in half

4 garlic cloves, peeled

2 eggplants, cut in half lengthwise

¼ cup plus 2 tablespoons olive oil

2 bird's-eye chilies, cut in half, seeds and ribs removed

1 teaspoon Harissa (page 16)

1 teaspoon ground cumin

Combine the chickpeas, carrot, and onion in a medium saucepan, add 4 cups water, and bring to a boil. Reduce the heat and simmer until the chickpeas are very tender, about 1½ hours. Drain, reserving 1 cup of the cooking liquid.

Meanwhile, preheat the oven to 300°F. Toss the garlic and eggplant with ¼ cup of the olive oil and arrange on a roasting pan, eggplant cut side down. Roast for 40 minutes. Add the chilies to the roasting pan, cut side down, and roast for another 10 minutes. Set aside until cool enough to handle.

Scoop the flesh from the eggplant and transfer to a blender. Add the roasted garlic and chilies, chickpeas, harissa, cumin, the remaining 2 tablespoons oil, and 2 to 3 tablespoons of the reserved cooking liquid. Puree, adding more cooking liquid 2 to 3 tablespoons at a time as necessary, until the mixture is smooth and creamy.

Serve at room temperature with warm pita bread.

MAKES 3 CUPS

DISCOVERY OF A CONTINENT

BEET-GINGER CHUTNEY

The natural sugars in beets lend a satisfying sweetness to this African-inspired chutney, while the ginger gives a pleasing bite. I like to serve it with the Harissa-Roasted Turkey Breast (page 126) because its lovely flavor and texture are an excellent complement to the bird.

2 tablespoons olive oil

4 shallots, finely chopped

4 garlic cloves, minced

Two 3-inch pieces ginger, peeled and sliced

4 beets, peeled and cut into ½-inch cubes

2 tablespoons honey

4 cardamom pods

2 thyme sprigs

2 tablespoons sugar

1 tablespoon Spiced Butter (page 20) or unsalted butter

2 cups chicken stock

½ teaspoon salt

Heat the oil in a large deep sauté pan over high heat. Add the shallots, garlic, ginger, and beets, reduce the heat to low, and sauté for 10 minutes, stirring occasionally.

Add the honey, cardamom, thyme, sugar, and spiced butter and stir over low heat for 1 minute. Add the chicken stock and bring to a simmer. Reduce the heat and simmer until beets are tender, 45 to 50 minutes.

Remove the cardamom, thyme, and ginger from the chutney and stir in the salt. Let cool.

Store in an airtight container in the refrigerator for up to 2 weeks.

MAKES 2 CUPS

PAPAYA KETCHUP

n Africa—where eating with your hands is an everyday experience—it's common to enrich the flavor of simple breads and grilled meats with a pungent dipping sauce. This one, which is laced with spicy serrano chilies, gets an exotic touch from the papaya. It makes a great accompaniment to grilled shrimp, chicken, and Roti (page 67).

2 teaspoons olive oil

1 garlic clove, minced

2 tomatoes, seeded and roughly chopped, or 1 cup chopped canned tomatoes

1 serrano chili, seeds and ribs removed, finely chopped

½ teaspoon sugar

1 tablespoon rice wine vinegar

1½ teaspoons soy sauce

½ teaspoon ground ginger

½ teaspoon Asian sesame oil

1 ripe papaya, peeled, seeded, and roughly chopped (about 1 cup)

Juice of 1 lime

Heat the olive oil in a large sauté pan over medium-high heat. Add the garlic and sauté for 2 to 3 minutes, until softened. Add the tomatoes, chili, sugar, and rice wine vinegar, reduce the heat to medium, and cook, stirring frequently, until the tomatoes are very soft, about 5 minutes. Remove from the heat and let cool slightly.

Transfer the tomato mixture to a blender. Add the soy sauce, ginger, sesame oil, papaya, and lime juice, and puree until smooth.

Store in a tightly covered container in the refrigerator for up to 5 days.

MAKES 2 CUPS

CHILI MAYONNAISE

While I was in Dakar, the capital of Senegal, I was surprised to see mayonnaise with nearly every meal. A holdover from the days of French rule, it is slathered on breakfast egg sandwiches, served as an accompaniment to meats and fish, and used in place of butter or olive oil as a dip for crusty French bread. In this version, I add some heat to an otherwise classic mayonnaise to bring in the African love of spiciness.

1 cup plus 1 tablespoon olive oil

1 tablespoon roughly chopped blanched almonds

2 garlic cloves, minced

2 serrano chilies, seeds and ribs removed, chopped

½ teaspoon chili powder

3 egg yolks

¼ cup fresh lime juice

2 teaspoons red wine vinegar

¾ cup canola oil

Salt and freshly ground black pepper

Heat 1 tablespoon of the olive oil in a small sauté pan over high heat. Add the almonds and garlic and sauté, stirring frequently, until golden brown, about 3 minutes. Lower the heat, add the chilies and chili powder, and cook just until the chilies begin to soften, about 2 minutes. Remove from the heat and set aside to cool.

Transfer the chili mixture to a blender, add the egg yolks, and blend well. Add the lime juice and vinegar and blend well. With the blender running, add the oil in a thin, steady stream and blend until well incorporated. Season with salt and pepper.

Store in a tightly covered container in the refrigerator for up to 3 days.

MAKES ABOUT 1⅓ CUPS

PIRI PIRI

Piri piri is the Swahili term for hot chili. It's also the name of the national dish of Mozambique, an extremely potent concoction used at tables around the country as a sauce for shellfish, fish, and chicken. Also known as pil pil and as pili pili, this fiery sauce is the first African food I ever had growing up in Sweden. In most cases, authentic piri piri is much too hot for American palates, so I've toned down the heat in this recipe. Because almost all of a chili pepper's heat is in the seeds and ribs, you can control the spiciness of the sauce by removing these hot spots or leaving them in, depending on your preference.

8 red bird's-eye chilies, seeds and ribs removed, chopped
½ cup fresh lemon juice
1 tablespoon chopped cilantro
1 tablespoon chopped parsley
2 garlic cloves
½ cup olive oil

Combine the chilies, lemon juice, cilantro, parsley, and garlic in a blender and puree until smooth. With the blender running, add the oil in a slow, steady stream and blend until well combined.

Store in an airtight container in the refrigerator for up to 2 weeks.

MAKES 1 CUP

PRESERVED CITRUS PEEL

Preserved lemons are an indispensable ingredient in Morocco, Algeria, and Tunisia, giving a fragrant, delicate citrus flavor to countless traditional dishes. This is a variation of the preserved lemons that are sold loose in souks (markets) throughout North Africa—the rinds of lemons, limes, oranges, and grapefruits are pickled in a sweet-salty solution for a mix of tart, sour, and sweet flavors. Don't skip any of the boiling and rinsing steps—the peel needs to be boiled in fresh water a total of three times to remove as much bitterness as possible.

2 lemons, scrubbed

2 limes, scrubbed

1 orange, scrubbed

1 grapefruit, scrubbed

1 cinnamon stick

1 tablespoon curry powder

1 red chili

1 teaspoon ground cardamom, preferably freshly ground

One 2-inch piece ginger, peeled and sliced

¼ cup salt

¼ cup honey

Using a sharp or serrated knife, cut away the colored peel from the lemons, limes, orange, and grapefruit, avoiding as much of the bitter white pith as possible. Reserve the fruit. Cut the peel into ½-inch-wide strips. Squeeze the juice from the fruit into a glass bowl; you should have about 2 cups of liquid. Set aside.

Place the peel and 2 cups water in a saucepan and bring to a boil; drain. Return the peel to the pan, add 2 cups of water, and bring to a boil; drain. Repeat once more, then drain.

Return the peel to the pan and add the reserved juice, the cinnamon stick, curry powder, chili, cardamom, ginger, salt, and honey. Bring to a boil, then reduce the heat and simmer for 5 to 6 minutes.

Remove from the heat and set aside to cool, then transfer to a quart jar or other container with a tight-fitting lid.

Store in a tightly sealed container in the refrigerator for up to 3 weeks.

MAKES 3 CUPS

BARBECUE SAUCE

Cooking outdoors over an open flame is a West African technique, but tomato-based barbecue sauces are an invention of the cooks of the American South, where there is intense competition in barbecue circles over the best recipes. My version features berbere and coffee, melding two quintessential Ethiopian ingredients with this all-American sauce for a fresh, new approach.

2 tablespoons olive oil

1 medium Spanish onion, diced

5 tomatoes, seeded and chopped, or 2½ cups chopped canned tomatoes

One 2-inch piece ginger, peeled and grated

3 garlic cloves, minced

1 serrano chili, seeds and ribs removed, finely chopped

2 cups water

¼ cup brewed coffee

1 tablespoon tamarind paste (see page 5)

2 teaspoons Berbere (page 8) or chili powder

¼ teaspoon ground cumin

¼ teaspoon coriander seeds, roughly crushed

¼ cup honey

Heat the oil in a large saucepan over high heat. Add the onion and sauté for 5 minutes, or until softened and translucent. Add the tomatoes, ginger, and garlic and bring to a simmer. Stir in the chili, water, coffee, tamarind paste, berbere, cumin, and coriander seeds and bring to a simmer. Reduce the heat and simmer for 40 minutes.

Add the honey and simmer for another 10 minutes, or until the sauce is thick enough to coat the back of a spoon. Let cool.

Store in a tightly covered container in the refrigerator for up to 5 days.

MAKES 2½ CUPS

MANGO SAMBAL

Where I grew up in Sweden, we have a tradition of serving sweet accompaniments with game and poultry. These jams and compotes are homey and comforting, but they tend to focus on one flavor note: sweetness. Here, I create a mango sambal with a hint of spiciness alongside the juicy sweet mango. I love serving this crisp-tasting condiment as an accompaniment to grilled fish, chicken, or meat.

¼ cup peanut oil

1 medium red onion, finely diced

2 garlic cloves, minced

¼ cup peanuts

One 2-inch piece ginger, peeled and grated

2 bird's-eye chilies, seeds and ribs removed, finely chopped

½ teaspoon chili powder

2 mangoes, peeled, pitted, and cut into 1-inch dice

2 mint sprigs, leaves only, chopped

2 teaspoons sesame seeds

1 teaspoon Asian sesame oil

Heat the peanut oil in a medium sauté pan over medium heat. Add the onion and garlic and sauté until the onion is translucent, about 5 minutes.

Add the peanuts, ginger, chilies, and chili powder and sauté until the peanuts are golden brown, about 5 minutes more. Remove from the heat and let cool.

Transfer the peanut mixture to a bowl and stir in the mangoes, mint, sesame seeds, and sesame oil.

Store in a tightly covered container in the refrigerator for up to 4 days.

MAKES 2½ CUPS

SAKAY

Over the past two thousand years, the island nation of Madagascar has been settled by a mix of African, Arab, Indonesian, and European peoples. All of them brought their own culinary influences and traditions, resulting in food that is full of flavor but simply prepared. Most recipes get a dose of heat from sakay, a fiery mash of dried red chilies, garlic, and ginger that is typically served on the side so diners can add as much or as little heat as they like.

¾ cup chili powder

1 tablespoon ground ginger

1½ teaspoons cayenne pepper

1 teaspoon ground cumin

4 garlic cloves, minced

2 teaspoons salt

1 cup peanut oil

Heat a medium sauté pan over medium heat. Add the chili powder, ginger, cayenne, cumin, and garlic and toast until fragrant, about 1 minute. Remove from the heat and let cool slightly.

Transfer the spice mixture to a blender, add the salt, and blend well on low speed. With the blender running, add the oil in a thin, steady stream and blend until a paste forms.

Store in the refrigerator in a tightly covered container for up to 2 weeks.

MAKES ABOUT 1⅓ CUPS

WHEN I WAS TWENTY-TWO AND fresh from Sweden, I visited Marrakech, during what would be one of the most important years of my culinary education. I was working on a luxury cruise ship that traveled the world, stopping at different ports of call along the way to pick up ingredients for the next day's meal.

Geographically, Morocco is very close to Europe, but the minute I set foot on the other side of the Mediterranean I knew I was in a completely different place. It had a mystique rooted in its culture that no European city has—I felt it in the ancient buildings, the elaborate, colorful mosaics that line the walls of mosques throughout the city, and the atmosphere that pervades the whole place. Marrakech is an old city, founded in the eleventh century, and donkeys and mules are still used to navigate streets too narrow for modern-day cars. The smells are distinctly earthy and evocative, and even the people look different—the men wear patterned baggy trousers and the women are swathed from head to toe in colorful fabrics and ornate jewelry.

But most memorable was the market in J'mal Fna, the city's old medina. It's a labyrinth lined with stalls that twists this way and that, and I lost my way a number of times as I wandered through the winding alleys. The streets were alive with shopkeepers and shoppers haggling over a jumble of leather goods, textiles, carpets, jewelry, food, clothing, and anything else you can imagine. On the sidelines, snake charmers, wildly whirling street dancers, fire eaters, and drummers competed for the attention of entranced tourists, while hurried locals plowed through this circuslike atmosphere in their rush to buy ingredients for that night's meal. There was a sense of urgency I'd never seen in a Western market, as if the people hurrying past wanted to say, "Get out of the way, things need to be sold, time is valuable."

I was an observer in this fascinating place, watching as an artisan in one corner of the market transferred brightly colored scarves and dresses from an enormous vat of dye set in the earth, while on the other side a shopkeeper weighed out salted lemons, spices, and olives. Around me, people bartered in a mishmash of languages, adding to the dreamlike sense of confusion. I felt like a foreigner and sensed that, in some way, I always would—that this was a culture I could never fully know or understand. It was both exhilarating and intimidating.

As for the food, it was a revelation. I'd read about ras al-hanout, the spice blend that Moroccan cuisine is built upon, but the exotic, intense hummus, breads, yogurt sauce, salted olives, and preserved lemons that we bought from vendors and ate in the street were as foreign to me as the veiled Muslim women who hurried through the market. This was my first taste of the beautifully balanced food of Morocco, with its delicate composition of couscous, rose water, pistachio, fragrant spices and dried fruits, and layers of seasonings reinforced in a beautiful composition of flavorful spreads, dips, and accompaniments.

My memories of that day in Marrakech are very cinematic. A bewildering, kaleidoscopic swirl of colors, sounds, tastes, and smells marked my entry to the alluring, mysterious Arab world.

THYME-ROASTED GARLIC

Roasting softens the harsh, assertive taste of raw garlic, giving it a delicate—almost sweet—taste that I like to use in sauces, dressings, dips, and many other dishes. To make more, just multiply the recipe to whatever amount you need.

1 head garlic
3 thyme sprigs
2 tablespoons peanut oil

Preheat the oven to 300°F. Cut off the top ½ inch of the garlic head. Place the garlic and thyme on a square of foil and drizzle with the peanut oil. Wrap the foil around the garlic and place on a small baking sheet.

Roast the garlic for 40 minutes, or until the cloves are softened. Discard the thyme, and let cool.

To use, squeeze the pulp from the papery skin.

To store, wrap tightly in plastic wrap and refrigerate for up to 3 days.

MAKES 1½ TABLESPOONS

TOMATO SAUCE

Often, tomato sauce tastes like a distant cousin of the gloriously ripe and flavorful tomatoes it is made from. Not in this version, which combines slow-roasted cherry tomatoes with juicy beefsteaks for an explosion of tomatoey taste and a great balance of flavor and texture. Only use fresh tomatoes in season, when they are at the peak of ripeness; at other times of the year, substitute canned tomatoes.

1 cup cherry tomatoes, cut in half

1 teaspoon sugar

1 teaspoon salt

2 teaspoons chopped thyme

½ cup olive oil, divided

4 garlic cloves, minced

One 2-inch piece ginger, peeled and sliced

½ cup peanuts

2 Scotch bonnet chilies, seeds and ribs removed, finely chopped

8 beefsteak or globe tomatoes, cut into quarters, or two 15-ounce cans tomatoes, chopped

Salt

1 tablespoon chopped parsley

Juice of 2 limes

Preheat the oven to 300°F. Combine the cherry tomatoes, sugar, salt, thyme, and 2 tablespoons of the olive oil in a medium bowl and toss to coat. Arrange the cherry tomatoes cut side up on a small baking sheet.

Roast the tomatoes until they begin to shrivel, about 40 minutes.

Meanwhile, heat the remaining 6 tablespoons olive oil in a large sauté pan over medium-high heat. Add the garlic, ginger, peanuts, and chilies and sauté until the garlic is golden brown, about 3 minutes. Add the beefsteak tomatoes and a pinch of salt, reduce the heat to low, and cook until the tomatoes have softened and released their liquid, about 15 minutes. Remove from the heat and let cool slightly.

Transfer the tomato-peanut mixture to a blender and puree until smooth. Pour into a large bowl.

Add the parsley, lime juice, and roasted cherry tomatoes to the sauce and stir well to combine. Season with salt to taste. Serve hot or at room temperature.

Store in a tightly covered container in the refrigerator for up to 3 days.

MAKES 6 CUPS

WHITE BEAN PUREE

Where I grew up, we used butter on our bread. But as I explored the foods of other cultures, I realized that you can have much more flavorful toppings, like this hummus-inspired white bean puree, which is great as a dip for bread or even as a spread on sandwiches. When you cook the beans, don't add salt, or they won't soften.

1 cup dried white cannellini beans, soaked in cold water for 8 hours and drained

2 slices bacon

4 garlic cloves, peeled

½ cup sliced portobello mushrooms

1 tablespoon unsalted butter

2 tablespoons extra-virgin olive oil

1 tablespoon freshly grated Parmesan cheese

Juice of 1 lime

Salt and freshly ground black pepper

Combine the beans, bacon, garlic, and mushrooms in a large pot, add water to cover by 1 to 1½ inches, and bring to a simmer. Simmer, uncovered, over low heat until the beans are soft, about 45 minutes.

Drain the beans and transfer to a food processor. Add the butter, oil, Parmesan cheese, and lime juice and process until smooth. Season with salt and pepper.

Store in a tightly covered container in the refrigerator for up to 3 days.

MAKES 3¾ CUPS

YOGURT DIP

Indian settlers in South Africa introduced a tangy dipping sauce that takes the heat off hot and spicy stews. Like the Greek tzatziki it reminds me of, it is yogurt-based with a creamy texture and a slightly sharp taste.

3 cups plain yogurt

2 tablespoons olive oil

2 garlic cloves, peeled

One 2-inch piece ginger, peeled and minced

1 jalapeño chili, seeds and ribs removed, finely chopped

½ teaspoon ground coriander

½ teaspoon ground cumin

Juice of 2 limes

2 teaspoons chopped cilantro

2 teaspoons chopped parsley

Salt and freshly ground black pepper

Set a fine-mesh sieve or colander lined with cheesecloth over a bowl. Add the yogurt, cover with plastic wrap, and let drain at room temperature for 2 to 3 hours, or refrigerate overnight.

Heat the olive oil in a medium saucepan over medium heat. Add the garlic, ginger, and jalapeño and sauté until the garlic is golden, about 5 minutes. Add the coriander and cumin and sauté until fragrant, about 2 minutes. Let cool briefly, then transfer to a blender, add the lime juice and drained yogurt, and blend until smooth.

Transfer to a bowl and fold in the cilantro and parsley. Season with salt and pepper.

Store in a tightly covered container in the refrigerator for up to 4 days.

MAKES 1½ CUPS

IN THE EUROPEAN- AND AMERICAN-STYLE COOKING that I grew up with, salads and side dishes are a complement to the main meal, made to balance and add another flavor to the entrée. But as I found on my travels, in many parts of Africa the approach is totally different: often, what we would consider a side dish is the meal. It's a different style that opens up some new and exciting ways to serve food.

Perhaps the most obvious example of this different approach is the North African tradition of meze, an inspired way to eat that stems from Middle Eastern traditions. A typical Moroccan meal could include a selection of salads, olives, and breads that lets you enjoy a range of wonderful flavors and textures while filling you up. But this tradition extends beyond the northern countries. South of the Sahara, much of the cooking is poor man's food based on one thing alone: to provide enough sustenance to get you through a day of hard work. Because of this, you find economical, hearty, stick-to-your-ribs staples that make the most of what is cheap and available: corn, yams, plantains, sweet potatoes, rice, cassava, beans. Farther south, no South African braai (a traditional barbecue) is complete without a rich selection of flavorful salads to accompany the grilled meats and sausages.

The recipes in this chapter use the variety of side dishes and salads I tried or heard about in my travels as a jumping-off point to create new classics. Whether you choose to enjoy these recipes as a traditional side to meat, fish, or poultry, or opt to serve a selection as the main part of the meal, they're a fun and flavorful way to bring African flavors to your table.

SALADS AND SIDES

CITRUS CABBAGE SALAD

At Aquavit, my philosophy toward creating new dishes has always been to take a slice of Scandinavian cooking—maybe using dill, or herring, or a pickling technique—to make a globally appealing dish. I do the same thing here with this pan-African recipe, which combines global flavors like soy sauce with common ingredients from around the continent, like peanuts and chilies. It's a great example of how African flavors can be incorporated into everyday cooking.

½ cup dry-roasted peanuts

One 2-inch piece ginger, peeled and grated

Juice of 2 limes

2 canned sardine fillets, chopped

1 garlic clove, minced

1 Scotch bonnet chili, seeds and ribs removed, chopped

¼ cup soy sauce

¼ cup peanut oil

1½ teaspoons Asian sesame oil

3 scallions, trimmed and chopped

1 tablespoon sesame seeds

½ head Napa cabbage, shredded (about 8 cups)

1 grapefruit, peel and white pith removed and segments sliced from membranes, juice reserved

Combine the peanuts and ginger in a medium sauté pan and sauté over medium heat until the peanuts begin to turn golden brown, about 2 minutes. Remove the pan from the heat and set aside to cool.

Transfer the peanuts and ginger to a blender, add the lime juice, sardines, garlic, chili, soy sauce, peanut oil, and sesame oil, and puree until smooth. Transfer to a large bowl.

Just before serving, stir the scallions and sesame seeds into the peanut mixture. Add the shredded cabbage and toss well. Fold in the grapefruit segments and juice. Serve immediately.

6 SERVINGS

SPICED EGG SALAD

The words "egg salad" may bring to mind a bland, mayonnaise-rich mash on soggy bread, but this spicy African-inflected version will put to rest any bad memories that conjures up. In addition to the heat from the chilies and paprika, I've added soy sauce for a salty note. It makes a great sandwich filling and is a crowd-pleasing addition to a buffet lunch.

¼ cup olive oil, divided
¼ cup unsalted blanched dry-roasted peanuts
1 bird's-eye chili, seeds and ribs removed, finely chopped
2 small red onions, finely chopped
3 garlic cloves, minced
1 tablespoon paprika
½ teaspoon ground ginger
1½ teaspoons chili powder
5 hard-boiled eggs, peeled and chopped
2 tomatoes, chopped
2 teaspoons chopped cilantro
1 tablespoon soy sauce
Juice of 1 lime
½ teaspoon salt

Heat 2 tablespoons of the olive oil in a large sauté pan over low heat. Add the peanuts and sauté until golden, about 5 minutes. Stir in the chilies, onions, and garlic and sauté until the onions are translucent, about 5 minutes. Add the paprika, ginger, and chili powder and cook until fragrant, about 2 minutes. Transfer to a bowl.

Gently fold in the eggs, tomatoes, cilantro, soy sauce, lime juice, the remaining 2 tablespoons olive oil, and the salt. Serve at room temperature.

6 SERVINGS

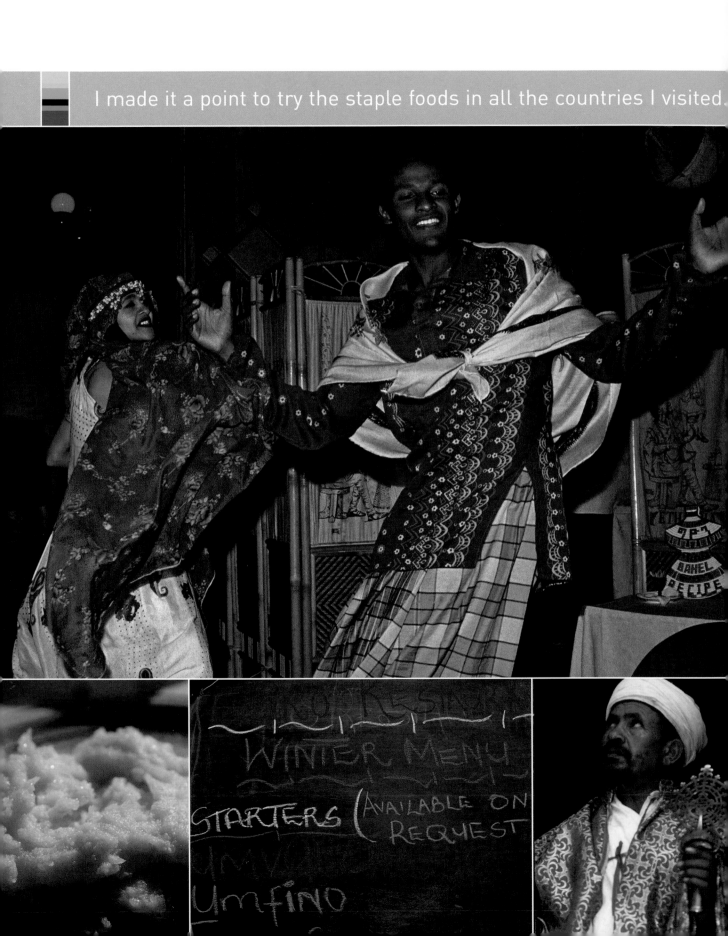

AS I TRAVELED THROUGH THE TANZANIAN mainland and Zanzibar, I asked the people I met what their favorite food was. To my surprise, I got the same answer from everyone: ugali. Ugali is served for breakfast, lunch, and dinner, and it is eaten by rolling a small chunk of cornmeal paste into a ball in the palm of your hand, then making an indentation with your thumb. The ball becomes a sort of edible spoon when you dip it into a stew or sauce and pop the whole thing into your mouth.

I had my first taste of ugali at a traditional Tanzanian buffet at the Peacock Hotel in Dar es Salaam and have to admit that its bland flavor and dull texture didn't make it onto my list of favorite foods. But I love learning about dishes like ugali, because it points out one of my favorite things about the cuisines of other cultures. Food is so much more than just taste: when you are raised with a food it becomes a part of who you are, with the power to comfort you.

Because of their appeal, I made it a point to try the staple foods in all the countries I visited. At Eziko's, a cooking school and restaurant outside of Cape Town that specializes in black South African cooking, I made mealie-pap, a cornmeal porridge also known as pap, by adding cornmeal to boiling water and cooking it until the water was absorbed. In Senegal, white rice or couscous made from cracked millet was served at every meal to accompany a variety of fish, meat, and vegetable stews. In other parts of West Africa, where fufu is the classic accompaniment to stews, I watched women patiently pounding boiled yams with a pestle or wooden spoon into a paste. Like ugali, that paste is then formed into small balls that are used as utensils to soak up sauce and scoop up pieces of meat, fish, or vegetables. While yams are the most common vegetable used for fufu, it is also made with cassava, plantains, green bananas, rice, beans, millet, sorghum, or cornmeal. In fact, fufu is so popular that I've even found boxes of fufu flour that make instant fufu at African markets here in the United States.

Like me, you may find that many of these staples are an acquired taste, but you can't help but appreciate that to millions of people around the continent these foods are a comforting source of nourishment that make an appearance at nearly every meal.

CORN MASHED POTATOES

C orn, introduced by European settlers to their colonies in Africa, has become an important food source in much of the continent, both used as a vegetable and dried and ground to make flour. Here, corn adds texture to a flavor-rich update of fufu, the staple vegetable mash served throughout West Africa.

1 small sweet potato (8 ounces), peeled
2 medium baking potatoes (1 pound), peeled
6 ears corn, shucked
1 cup coconut milk
2 tablespoons olive oil
2 tablespoons Spiced Butter (page 20) or unsalted butter
1½ teaspoons garam masala
½ teaspoon salt

Combine the sweet potato and baking potatoes in a large pot, add water to cover, and bring to a boil. Boil until tender, about 30 minutes. Five minutes before the potatoes are done, add the corn.

Drain the potatoes and corn and transfer the potatoes to a large bowl. Set the corn aside to cool slightly, and mash the potatoes with a fork. Cut the corn kernels from the cobs, and fold into the potatoes.

Combine the coconut milk, olive oil, and spiced butter in a small saucepan and bring to a boil. Stir the flavored coconut milk into the mashed potatoes, then add the garam masala and salt and mix well.

6 SERVINGS

CRISPY AVOCADO

These tasty bites showcase the silken richness of avocado. The success of the recipe lies in choosing the right avocados. Look for those that are still slightly firm and "give" just a little when you squeeze them, because as they are fried they will soften up. Avoid avocados that are overly ripe, which will either fall apart when cooked this way or become mushy.

2 tablespoons cornstarch
1½ teaspoons Berbere (page 8)
4 large egg whites
About 4 cups peanut oil for deep-frying
3 ripe but firm avocados, pitted, peeled, and cut into quarters
Juice of 3 limes
4 cilantro sprigs, chopped
¼ teaspoon salt

Mix together the cornstarch and berbere on a plate. Whisk the egg whites together in a large shallow bowl.

Heat the oil to 350°F in a deep saucepan. While the oil heats, dredge the avocado slices in the cornstarch mixture, then add the pieces to the egg whites. Working in batches, carefully add the avocados to the hot oil and fry until golden brown, about 4 minutes. Drain on paper towels, then transfer to a serving plate.

Drizzle the lime juice over the avocados. Sprinkle with the cilantro and salt and serve immediately.

4 SERVINGS

MANGO COUSCOUS

Muna, an acquaintance from Libya, tells of visiting her aunt back home and sitting outside with her and the neighborhood women as they made couscous. She described the hypnotic process of the women rolling semolina dough in their hands, crumbling it into smaller chunks with their fingers, then rubbing the crumbs into smaller pieces until they were the right size. They made huge batches at a time, laying the grains in the sun to dry, then steaming them and drying them again. Fortunately, commercially made couscous is easy to find in stores and of very high quality, so you can enjoy this lovely dish without spending days preparing the grains.

1 cup couscous

2 tablespoons olive oil, divided

1 garlic clove, minced

1 mango, peeled, pitted, and cut into 1-inch cubes (about 1 cup)

1 jalapeño chili, seeds and ribs removed, finely chopped

½ cup raisins

1 ripe tomato, chopped

Juice of 1 lime

¼ cup loosely packed small cilantro sprigs, chopped

¼ cup loosely packed small parsley sprigs, chopped

Salt

Prepare the couscous according to the package directions. Set aside.

Heat 1 tablespoon of the olive oil in a large sauté pan over high heat. Add the garlic, mango, and jalapeño and sauté until the mango begins to color lightly. Stir in the remaining tablespoon of olive oil, the couscous, raisins, tomato, lime juice, cilantro, and parsley and toss to heat through. Season with salt.

Serve hot or at room temperature.

4 SERVINGS

WARM EGGPLANT-BUTTERNUT SQUASH SALAD

My friend Hamid is originally from Morocco and has an encyclopedic knowledge of the foods of his homeland. He told me about one of his favorite meze, a warm salad made of eggplant and squash, known as zalouk. I've adapted his traditional recipe, adding the warm flavor of sumac and some zesty chilies to create a distinctive new meze that is an excellent appetizer when paired with pita, or a satisfying side to any roasted meat dish.

1½ tablespoons sumac (see page 5)

½ cup olive oil, divided

2 small butternut squash, peeled, seeded, and cut into 1-inch cubes (about 6 cups)

2 medium eggplants, peeled and cut into 2-inch cubes (about 6 cups)

One 3-inch piece ginger, peeled and sliced

Finely chopped zest of 1 lemon

6 garlic cloves, minced

2 red chilies, seeds and ribs removed, finely chopped

⅓ cup honey

½ cup water

1½ cups loosely packed baby spinach leaves

Juice of 2 limes

1 tablespoon chopped parsley

Salt

Preheat the oven to 350°F. Combine the sumac with 7 tablespoons of the olive oil in a small bowl. Toss the squash with half the oil, spread on a baking sheet in a single layer, and roast for about 40 minutes, until tender. After the squash has cooked for 15 minutes, toss the eggplant with the remaining oil and spread in a single layer on a second baking sheet. Place in the oven and roast until tender, about 25 minutes.

Meanwhile, heat the remaining 1 tablespoon olive oil in a large sauté pan over low heat. Add the ginger, lemon zest, garlic, and chilies and sauté until fragrant, about 5 minutes. Add the honey and water, stir to combine, and bring to a simmer. Simmer for 5 minutes. Remove from the heat and set aside.

Remove the vegetables from the oven and transfer to a large bowl. Add the spinach, the chili mixture, lime juice, and parsley and toss until the spinach wilts slightly. Season with salt.

4 TO 6 SERVINGS

POMEGRANATE RICE

art, refreshing pomegranates have grown in Africa at least since the time of Moses and were so well loved that they even got a mention in the book of Deuteronomy. Since then, this gorgeous fruit has spread around the globe, lending great texture and color to many global dishes. Here, I combine pomegranates with rice. The secret to this dish is to cook part of the rice in butter to make it crunchy, giving another nice texture along with the pomegranate seeds.

2 tablespoons Spiced Butter (page 20) or unsalted butter
2 cups broken jasmine rice or long-grain white rice
½ cup olive oil
2 shallots, chopped
One 2-inch piece ginger, peeled and grated
1 cinnamon stick
3 cups chicken stock
1 bay leaf
½ cup pistachios
Seeds from 2 pomegranates

Melt the butter in a medium sauté pan over very low heat. Add ½ cup of the rice, stirring to coat. Cook for 30 minutes, stirring occasionally, until the rice is a nut-brown color. Remove from the heat.

Meanwhile, heat the oil in a medium saucepan over medium heat. Add the shallots, ginger, cinnamon, and the remaining 1½ cups rice and sauté, stirring frequently, until the rice is golden brown, about 5 minutes. Add the chicken stock and bay leaf and bring to a boil. Reduce the heat, cover, and simmer for 14 minutes. Remove from the heat and let sit, covered, for 10 minutes, or until all the liquid is absorbed.

Mix together the rices in a bowl, and fold in the pistachios and pomegranate seeds.

Remove the bay leaf. Serve immediately or at room temperature.

6 SERVINGS

DISCOVERY OF A CONTINENT

RED RICE

n Dakar I was served a rice dish that had a startlingly vivid red hue and a pleasingly intense flavor. The color and taste came from shrimp powder, made from dried shrimp pounded by hand to a fine, dusty powder, then sifted to remove any shells. Shrimp powder has limited availability in the United States, but it's worth seeking out at African or Asian markets. If you can't find it, you can get a similar color by adding a tablespoon of tomato paste along with the tomato juice.

¼ cup peanut oil

1 small red onion, sliced

1 jalapeño chili, seeds and ribs removed, finely chopped

2 teaspoons shrimp powder (optional)

3 garlic cloves, minced

2 tomatoes, chopped, or 1 cup chopped canned tomatoes

1 teaspoon chili powder

1 cup short-grain white rice

1½ teaspoons salt

2 thyme sprigs

1 cup tomato juice

2 cups water

¼ cup loosely packed cilantro sprigs, chopped

Heat the peanut oil in a large saucepan over high heat. When the oil shimmers, add the onion and cook until translucent, 5 to 7 minutes. Add the jalapeño, shrimp powder, if using, and garlic and sauté for 1 minute. Reduce the heat to low, stir in the tomatoes and chili powder, and cook for 10 minutes, or until the oil separates from the tomatoes.

Add the rice and stir to coat. Stir in the salt, thyme, tomato juice, and water and bring to a boil. Reduce the heat to low, cover, and simmer for 15 minutes.

Remove the pan from the heat and stir in the cilantro. Replace the cover and let sit for 10 minutes, until all the liquid is absorbed.

4 TO 6 SERVINGS

SPICY PLANTAIN CHIPS

Plantains, the large, starchy cousin of the banana, are a staple throughout Africa and used in much the same way as potatoes are here. These chips make an excellent snack before a meal. Deep-fried plantains can often be a little dull and starchy, but by frying them in spiced butter and oil, and dusting them with a spicy curry powder, they get a lively, complex flavor. Green, unripe plantains make the best chips because they are firmer and hold up better during cooking.

2 green plantains
1 tablespoon curry powder
1 teaspoon confectioners' sugar
1 teaspoon salt
1 cup Spiced Butter (page 20) or ½ pound (2 sticks) unsalted butter
About 2 cups canola oil

Peel the plantains (see page 4) and slice as thin as possible with a mandoline, peeler, or sharp knife. Place in a bowl, cover with cold water, and let soak for 10 minutes to wash away excess starch. (The starch can cause the slices to stick together during frying.) Drain, rinse, and blot thoroughly dry with paper towels.

Meanwhile, combine the curry powder, sugar, and salt in a small bowl.

Melt the spiced butter in a large deep pot over medium heat, then add enough oil to come to a depth of 1½ inches. Increase the heat to medium-high and heat the oil to 350°F. Working in batches, carefully lower the plantains into the oil with a slotted spoon and fry, stirring occasionally to prevent the slices from sticking together, until evenly browned, about 4 minutes. Remove from the oil and drain on paper towels. Dust with the curry and sugar mixture and serve immediately.

MAKES ABOUT 2½ CUPS

TRAVELING THROUGH AFRICA is a bit like taking a greatest-bread-hits-of-the-world tour: in Morocco I tore into Middle Eastern-style pitas and flatbreads, in Tanzania I dipped Indian chapatis into stews and sauces, in South Africa I tasted traditional Zulu steamed bread, and in Senegal I met up with two familiar favorites, the French baguette and croissant.

Breads play an important role in African cooking, where they are just as valued for their taste as they are for their belly-filling capabilities. In some places breads take the place of utensils, used to scoop up stews and dips and sauces. Breads are cheap and flavorful, making them an important part of the daily meal in places where finding economical solutions is a necessity.

African cooks take inexpensive meats and proteins and stretch them to create a mind-bogglingly diverse range of sandwiches and soups. As I was on the run in Africa, I found myself stopping at roadside vendors for a quick bite to tide me over, like the tripe soup I spooned up in an abandoned lot in Soweto, or the samosas I had in Cape Town's Muslim Bo-Kaap district.

The global flavors of African breads and sandwiches inspired the recipes in this chapter. Try a Crab Burger when you want a break from a run-of-the-mill ham and cheese sandwich. As for the breads, add a touch of the continent to your next dinner party by dispensing with utensils and letting your guests dip roti in the stew to scoop up delicious tidbits and flavorful broth, bringing the laid-back and relaxed atmosphere of Africa into your dining room.

BREADS AND SANDWICHES

CORN BREAD

West African food took on a life of its own when it was transplanted to the United States, evolving into the soul food you find all over the country today. I remember going to gospel brunches in Harlem when I first moved to New York, and how I immediately loved the corn bread. It's made in all forms—sweetened or unsweetened, flavored or not, muffins, loaves, or slices—and I like them all.

This is a semisweet version that gets a little kick from the chilies and chili powder, and is mellowed by smooth honey. Serve it warm from the oven with soups, stews, or any other rustic dishes to sop up the gravy or juices.

1 small ear of corn, shucked

¾ cup milk

1 package active dry yeast (2¼ teaspoons)

1 tablespoon unsalted butter

1 jalapeño chili, seeds and ribs removed, finely chopped

2 scallions, trimmed and chopped

1 teaspoon chili powder

1 cup all-purpose flour

1 cup cornmeal

1 teaspoon salt

3 tablespoons honey

1 egg

Cut the kernels from the corncob; break the corncob in half and reserve. Combine the milk, corncob, and corn in a small saucepan and bring to a boil. Remove from the heat and let cool until just warm. Whisk in the yeast, cover, and let sit for 10 minutes.

Meanwhile, heat the butter in a small saucepan over high heat until it starts to foam and then the foam subsides. Add the jalapeño, scallions, and chili powder and sauté until the jalapeño is softened and the scallions are wilted, about 5 minutes. Remove from the heat and set aside to cool.

Stir the flour, cornmeal, and salt together in a large bowl. Make a well in the center and pour in the corn-milk mixture, then slowly stir the liquid into the flour until all the liquid has been absorbed. Stir in the honey, egg, and jalapeño-scallion mixture.

Turn the dough onto a lightly floured work surface and knead until smooth and elastic. Transfer the dough to a clean bowl, cover with a damp cloth or oiled plastic wrap, and let rise in a warm, draft-free place until risen to 1½ times its original size, about 45 minutes.

Preheat the oven to 375°F. Punch down the dough and shape it into a loaf. Place in an 8½ x 4½-inch loaf pan, and bake for 35 to 40 minutes, until the bread is golden on top and a toothpick inserted in the center of the loaf comes out clean. Let cool for 5 minutes.

Turn the loaf out onto a cooling rack and let cool for 10 minutes. Cut into ½-inch slices and serve warm.

MAKES 1 LOAF

AFRICAN SWEET MORNING ROLLS

Starbucks store manager Denise Vigil's passion for cooking led her to The Culinary Institute of America, where she fell in love with the history, the chemistry, and the art of cooking.

"I spent my twenties working in restaurants around the country. It was an exciting time, cooking in the kitchens with James Beard Award–winning chefs. Now, I have a three-year-old daughter and the days of preparing three-hour dinners are behind me, but I haven't lost my passion for cooking. To me, a recipe is a map that gives directions to a taste destination; along the way, it tells the story of a place or time. With this recipe, I've created the taste of an African morning. These rolls are a beautiful complement to Starbucks' African coffee blends, my personal favorite of all the varieties available."

SWEET ROLLS

1 cup whole milk
¼ cup unsweetened coconut milk
4 tablespoons (½ stick) butter
2 tablespoons sugar
1 ¼-ounce package instant yeast
2¼ cups all-purpose flour
1¼ cups millet flour (or additional all-purpose flour)
1½ teaspoons salt
2 large eggs
½ teaspoon vanilla

DATE-CURRANT FILLING

¼ cup packed light brown sugar
⅔ cup chopped pitted dates
¼ cup finely chopped almonds
¼ cup currants
1 tablespoon grated lemon or orange zest
1 teaspoon ground cinnamon
⅛ teaspoon ground cardamom
⅛ teaspoon ground cloves
6 tablespoons (¾ stick) butter, softened

COFFEE ICING

1 cup powdered sugar
2 tablespoons brewed Ethiopian Sidamo coffee, at room temperature
1½ teaspoons orange juice

To make the dough: Combine the milk, coconut milk, butter, and sugar in a medium saucepan and stir over medium heat until the butter is nearly melted and the mixture is warm (115°F). Remove from the heat and stir in the yeast. Let stand for 10 minutes, or until the yeast is foamy.

In a large bowl, combine the all-purpose flour, millet flour, and salt and make a well in the center. Add the eggs and vanilla to the milk mixture, and pour the liquid into the well in the flour. Stir just until all the ingredients are fully incorporated; do not overmix, or the rolls will not be tender. Cover the dough and let rise in a warm place until doubled in size, about 1 hour.

Punch the dough down. Turn out onto a lightly floured surface and divide in half. Cover and let rest for 10 minutes.

Meanwhile, make the filling: Combine all the ingredients except the butter in a bowl and mix well.

Butter two 9 x 13-inch baking dishes or pans. On a lightly floured surface, gently pat each half of the dough into a 12 x 10-inch rectangle. Spread each rectangle with 3 tablespoons of the softened butter, and sprinkle half of the filling mixture evenly over each half. Starting from a long side, roll up each rectangle jelly-roll style.

Cut each roll into 12 slices. Place the slices cut side down in the prepared pans. Cover and let rise in a warm place until almost doubled in size, about 30 minutes.

Preheat the oven to 375°F.

Bake the rolls for 20 minutes, or until golden brown.

While the rolls are baking, make the icing: Whisk together all the ingredients in a small bowl until smooth.

Drizzle the icing over the warm rolls. Serve warm.

MAKES 2 DOZEN ROLLS

HONEY BREAD

n the land of milk and honey, injera may be the staple, but it is not the only kind of bread. In the morning, it's dabo—honey bread—that graces the Ethiopian breakfast table. Unlike the pancakelike injera, dabo is a European-style loaf that is typically slathered with shiro, a chickpea spread. It highlights one of the distinctive characteristics of Ethiopian cooking: sweeteners are very rarely used, but an element of sweetness is introduced through other means, such as sugary coffees and teas; tej, a syrupy honey wine; or this dense breakfast bread, which lends a gentle sweetness to the start of the day.

1 tablespoon chopped rosemary
¼ cup canola oil
2 packets active dry yeast (1½ tablespoons)
2½ cups warm water
7 cups all-purpose flour
1 tablespoon salt
6 cups honey

Toast the rosemary in a small sauté pan over medium-high heat until fragrant, about 30 seconds. Remove from the heat and set aside.

In a small bowl, combine the oil, yeast, and warm water and stir to dissolve the yeast. Let sit for 5 minutes, or until foamy.

Combine the flour and salt and mound in a large bowl. Make a well in the middle. Slowly pour the dissolved yeast into the well, working in the flour with your fin-gertips, then knead the dough until a ball forms. Knead in the honey and toasted rosemary.

Put the dough in a large oiled bowl and turn to coat. Cover with a damp cloth or oiled plastic wrap and let rise to 1½ times the original size, about 1 hour.

Grease two 9 x 4-inch loaf pans. Punch down the dough and transfer to a floured work surface. Knead for 5 minutes. Divide the dough in half and shape into loaves. Place in the prepared pans, cover with plastic wrap, and let rise for 20 minutes.

Preheat the oven to 400°F. Place the pans in the oven and bake until the tops are golden, about 25 to 30 min-utes. Invert the pans onto a cooling rack and let sit for 5 minutes, then remove the pans and let cool.

MAKES 2 LOAVES

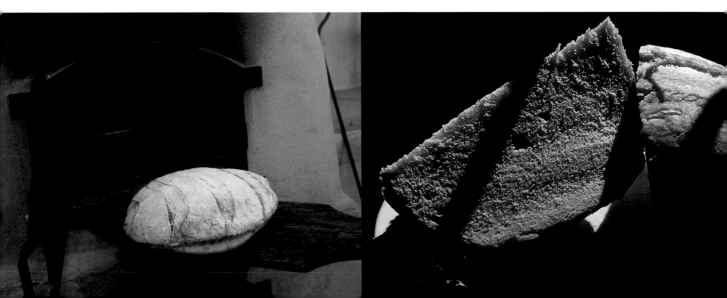

ROTI

Travelers to East Africa are often surprised to find Indian curries and breads served there. This region has a long history of trade with India, and many of that country's flavors and cooking techniques have been incorporated into the local cuisine. It's common to buy Indian-style samosas, fritters, and breads from the popular street vendors. This is my favorite roti, flavored with curry and coconut milk, and deep-fried so it puffs as it cooks, giving it a crispy exterior and a soft, chewy inside. Serve this unleavened savory bread with stews to soak up extra juices, or with a dipping sauce like Papaya Ketchup (page 32).

2 tablespoons curry powder

2 teaspoons salt

2 tablespoons confectioners' sugar

3 cups all-purpose flour

1 large egg

1 egg yolk

½ cup coconut milk

¼ cup chicken stock

1 tablespoon canola oil, plus about 4 cups for deep-frying

Combine the curry powder, salt, sugar, and flour in a large bowl, and make a deep well in the center. Whisk the egg and egg yolk together, then pour into the well. Add the coconut milk, chicken stock, and 1 tablespoon canola oil and slowly stir until all the liquid has been absorbed and the dough forms a ball.

Transfer the dough to a lightly floured work surface and knead until smooth and elastic, 10 to 15 minutes. Shape the dough into a ball, then cover with a damp cloth and let rest for 30 minutes.

On a lightly floured surface, roll out the dough to a large ½-inch-thick rectangle. Cut into 2 x 4-inch strips.

Heat 3 inches of canola oil in a deep pot to 350°F. Working in batches, carefully drop the dough strips into the oil, stirring to keep them from sticking together. The bread will puff and rise to the surface. Fry until brown and crisp, about 2 to 3 minutes, turning once to brown both sides. Transfer to paper towels to drain. Serve immediately.

MAKES 24 PIECES

CORIANDER–SWEET POTATO SCONES WITH PEPPER-LIME BUTTER

Katy Branson, a Starbucks store manager in Tennessee, loves to bake. Sometimes it takes several tries to get the recipe right, but for Katy, giving people something you made lets them know how special they are.

"Sweet potatoes are an African food, but are also very closely linked with my southern cooking traditions. With these scones, it took over a dozen tries to get the right texture without sacrificing the subtle flavor of the sweet potato. The coriander balances the sweet potato well and adds a little exoticism to an otherwise simple recipe."

Freshly ground coriander has a sweet, citrus-like flavor that dissipates quickly when stored, so if possible, grind your own coriander seeds with a mortar and pestle, or a very clean coffee grinder. These are best the day they are made.

CORIANDER–SWEET POTATO SCONES

3 cups all-purpose flour

2 teaspoons baking powder

½ teaspoon salt

2 teaspoons ground coriander, preferably freshly ground

8 tablespoons (1 stick) butter, cut into cubes and chilled

2 large eggs

⅓ cup plus 2 tablespoons whole milk

1 cup mashed (cooked) sweet potatoes

PEPPER-LIME BUTTER

4 tablespoons (½ stick) butter, softened

½ teaspoon coarsely ground black pepper

½ teaspoon grated lime zest

1 teaspoon fresh lime juice

To make the scones: Preheat the oven to 425°F.

Put the flour, baking powder, salt, and coriander in a processor and pulse to blend. Add butter and pulse until the consistencey of fine cornmeal.

In a small bowl, whisk the eggs just to mix, then whisk in ⅓ cup of the milk and the sweet potato. With the food processor running, add the sweet potato mixture and process just until the dough combines into a ball, 30 to 60 seconds.

Turn the dough out onto a well-floured surface and divide into 4 pieces. Pat each piece into a 6-inch circle, and cut each circle into 4 wedges. Place 1 inch apart on an ungreased baking sheet. Brush with the remaining 2 tablespoons milk. Bake for 18 to 20 minutes, until golden.

While the scones bake, make the pepper-lime butter: In a small bowl, blend the butter, pepper, lime zest, and lime juice well with a fork. Do not refrigerate.

Serve the scones hot, with the butter.

MAKES 16 SCONES

FRIED FISH BAGUETTE

n Zambia, it's common to see older ladies selling whole fried fish, head and all, from stalls in the market. In this recipe I use fillets, which are much more manageable in a sandwich, and give it a dose of heat with chili mayonnaise and harissa.

½ cup white wine vinegar
½ cup water
1½ teaspoons sugar
1 jalapeño chili, seeds and ribs removed, thinly sliced
2 garlic cloves, thinly sliced
2 tomatoes, thinly sliced
Eight 4-ounce black bass fillets, cut in half
2 teaspoons Harissa (page 16)
2 tablespoons olive oil
2 tablespoons Chili Mayonnaise (page 32)
2 baguettes, split lengthwise
1 teaspoon Dijon mustard
1 head Bibb lettuce, leaves separated, rinsed, and dried
4 to 6 lime wedges

To make the pickled tomatoes, combine the vinegar, water, sugar, chili, and garlic in a medium saucepan and bring to a boil. Add the tomatoes and simmer for 2 minutes. Remove from the heat and let cool.

Toss the fish with the harissa. Heat a large sauté pan over high heat. Add the olive oil and heat until shimmering. Working in batches, add the fish and sear for 2 minutes on each side.

Meanwhile, spread the chili mayonnaise on the cut sides of the bread. Spread the mustard on the top cut side. Layer the bottom half with the lettuce leaves.

Divide the fish fillets between the two baguettes, layering them on top of the lettuce. Top the fish with the pickled tomatoes and cover with the baguette tops. Cut each loaf into 3-inch pieces, and serve with lime wedges.

4 TO 6 SERVINGS

IN CASABLANCA, EVERYBODY WENT TO RICK'S, but when you are in Soweto—the sister city of Johannesburg—Wandie's Place is the place to be. Wandie's is one of the most famous restaurants in Africa, attracting foreign politicians, visiting celebrities, and busloads of tourists who come for the delicious black South African fare and the charming company of owner Wandie Ndaba. But it wasn't always this way. Today Wandie's may be the local hot spot, but like everything I saw in Soweto, the restaurant has evolved over the years to fit into the ever-changing neighborhood that surrounds it.

Wandie's began in 1981 as an illegal local shebeen (saloon) run out of Wandie's house. At the time, Soweto, which is short for "South Western Townships," was a hotbed of anti-apartheid activities—it's the only place in the world with one street where two Nobel peace prize winners, Desmond Tutu and Nelson Mandela, once lived—and Wandie's was in constant danger of being shut down by a police raid. By 1991, as apartheid was coming to its inevitable end, Wandie received a license for his joint and began serving food, carving out a niche for himself in the new up-and-coming neighborhood. As his restaurant gained popularity, Wandie added an extension to his house to accommodate the hundreds of locals and tourists who come to eat every day. Today, Wandie is one of South Africa's leading celebrity chefs, but remarkably he has maintained the intimate feeling of a shebeen at his restaurant, welcoming each guest as a long awaited friend. Visitors make their mark on the restaurant, too, signing the wall or hanging their business cards next to signed photos of visiting luminaries like Bill Clinton, Quincy Jones, and Richard Branson.

The day I visited Wandie's began with an early morning trip to Soweto's Baragwanath market, a huge bus terminal lined with stalls selling food. Nearly every vendor sells a packaged breakfast featuring a grilled bologna sandwich, a hard-boiled egg, and pork sausage. Once the workers were on their way, the vendors transformed their stalls' offerings to a selection of chips, candy, vegetables, and cups of sweetened rooibos, red bush tea with dried milk and sweetened condensed milk. Then we set off for Wandie's.

My visit began with drinks on the patio, sipping gemmer (ginger beer) and mageu (a yogurtlike drink traditionally given to guests when they enter the home) while Wandie entertained me with stories of his past. A cheerful, welcoming man who is proud of his Xhosa heritage, Wandie then surprised me with a bowl of dried mopane, sun-dried caterpillars harvested from the leaves of a local tree. They are loaded with protein, making them a nutrient-dense staple for rural tribes in South Africa and Zimbabwe, but they are truly an acquired taste. Wandie laughed at my efforts to be polite about the worms, then gave the bowl to his young son, who cheerfully devoured the rest.

Happily, the rest of our lunch was more appealing to me. Wandie has a team of local women cooking in his kitchen, and they dished up a delicious array of traditional foods: curries, roasted meats, stews, vegetables, salads, and steamed bread, a Zulu specialty. All the food at Wandie's is served buffet-style, and I went through the line helping myself to mutton curry, roasted lamb, fried chicken, pumpkin mash, grilled sweet potatoes, and tomato "gravy." I also tried samp, the white corn and bean porridge that Wandie told me is Nelson Mandela's favorite whenever he visits the restaurant. I sat in the dining room sipping a glass of Cape pinotage, and was soon joined by a group of local businessmen who chatted about everything from their own lives growing up in a much different Soweto to the chances of South Africa's attracting the 2010 World Cup championship. (They did.) As I temporarily joined into this delightful part of South African life, I saw what a hopeful time this was for a country that had turned its back on a sad and difficult past to embrace a promising future where everyone has an equal chance.

CRAB BURGERS

One of my favorite food memories is from a trip I took to Trinidad and Tobago to visit my friend Wendy, who had moved back to Port of Spain after a few years in New York. She drove me to Maracas Beach, about forty minutes outside of the city, where all the shacks along the beach sold the same thing: "bake 'n' shark," a grilled fish sandwich that Wendy loves. We placed our order with one of the vendors, then watched as he grilled the fish, fried the bread, and dressed our sandwiches with garlic sauce and chado benny (a condiment made from a cilantrolike herb, vinegar, and rum-pickled chilies). Sitting on the beach washing the sandwiches down with a cold Caribe beer was one of those perfect moments that come only when you're traveling. A regular vacationer might just dream about going back to that place, but the chef in me wants to re-create those moments, as I do with this Crab Burger.

2 garlic cloves, minced

1 jalapeño chili, seeds and ribs removed, finely chopped

¼ cup chopped cilantro

1 cup cooked black beans, rinsed if canned

½ teaspoon salt

1½ pounds jumbo lump crabmeat, picked over for shells and cartilage

2 cups plus 2 tablespoons all-purpose flour

2 tablespoons olive oil

Combine the garlic, jalapeño, cilantro, beans, and salt in a food processor and puree until smooth. Transfer the puree to a bowl and gently fold in the crabmeat and 2 tablespoons of the flour.

Spread the remaining 2 cups flour on a plate. With wet hands, to prevent sticking, shape the crab mixture into 6 patties, 4 inches in diameter and 1 inch thick. Dredge the patties in the flour, shaking off any excess.

Heat the olive oil in a large sauté pan over medium heat. When the oil starts to shimmer, add the patties, in batches if necessary, and cook for 4 minutes on each side.

Serve at room temperature on toasted buns, with Chili Mayonnaise (page 32), Mango Sambal (page 37), and Papaya Ketchup (page 32).

6 SERVINGS

CHILI-SPICED LAMB SANDWICHES

When I was growing up in Sweden, my parents very rarely let my sisters and me eat at fast food restaurants. But they had no issue with our eating the takeout sandwiches sold by recent immigrants from the Middle East and eastern Africa. This lamb sandwich, served with a sauce deliciously tart with lemon and tangy with olives and mint, is typical of those I ate as a boy and later saw on my travels through North Africa, where lamb is the most common meat.

2 tablespoons Harissa (page 16)

½ cup olive oil

1½ pounds boneless lamb loin, cut into 1-inch cubes

1 medium red onion, sliced

1½ cup chicken stock or water

2 lemons, cut into quarters

1 cup chickpeas, soaked in cold water for 24 hours and drained

4 tomatoes, diced, or 2 cups chopped canned tomatoes

2 cinnamon sticks

4 garlic cloves, cut into thirds

½ cup fresh lemon juice

½ cup black olives, pitted and cut in half

4 mint sprigs, leaves only, minced

Salt and freshly ground black pepper

2 pita breads, warmed

Chickpea-Eggplant Dip (page 26)

Mix the harissa and olive oil in a large bowl. Add the lamb cubes and toss to coat.

Heat a large sauté pan over high heat. Add the lamb and onion and sear on all sides, about 3 minutes per side. Remove the lamb from the pan with a slotted spoon.

Add the chicken stock, lemons, chickpeas, tomatoes, cinnamon, and garlic to the same pan and stir well. Bring to a simmer, stirring with a wooden spoon to scrape up any browned bits on the bottom of the pan. Reduce the heat and simmer, uncovered, for 25 minutes.

Return the lamb to the pan, add the lemon juice and olives, and simmer for 5 minutes. Stir in the mint and cook for 2 more minutes. Remove the cinnamon sticks, and season with salt and pepper. Remove from the heat.

Slice the pita breads in half. Spread the dip inside each pocket, and, using a slotted spoon, stuff the pockets with the lamb and vegetables.

4 SERVINGS

EGG SANDWICHES

Many people stay away from street food when they are traveling. Not me. I love experiencing a culture through its street food, because it gives me insight that I'd never find at fancier, tourist-oriented restaurants. One morning after an early jog on the beach in Dakar, I stopped at one of the local food stands for breakfast. The owner served just one thing—an egg sandwich—from his stand, which consisted of a table with a gas-fired burner, a coffee kettle, and a few chairs. Men stood in line for their coffee and sandwiches, then sat down at a little table nearby to eat and converse before going to work. I thought it was a perfectly delicious way to start the day.

2 tomatoes, thinly sliced
¼ head iceberg lettuce, shredded
2 small red onions, 1 sliced, 1 cut into ¼-inch dice
6 large eggs
¾ cup milk
½ teaspoon chili powder
½ teaspoon salt
2 tablespoons canola oil
2 tablespoons Chili Mayonnaise (page 32)
1 baguette, split lengthwise and cut into quarters

Combine the tomatoes, lettuce, and sliced onion in a bowl. Set aside.

Whisk the eggs, diced onion, milk, chili powder, and salt together in a separate bowl. Heat 1 tablespoon of the oil in a large sauté pan over high heat. Add half the egg mixture and stir until the eggs are set, then flip and cook on the other side until golden brown. Transfer to a warmed plate and repeat with the remaining eggs.

Spread a thin layer of mayonnaise on the cut sides of the baguette. Divide the eggs in half, and put on the bottom halves of the bread. Top with the tomato, lettuce, and onion and serve.

4 SERVINGS

DISCOVERY OF A CONTINENT

LAMB AND VEAL KEFTA WITH TOMATO-CUCUMBER SALAD

Morocco is a friendly, frenzied, energizing place—open-air bazaars are everywhere, crowded with stalls selling stunning rugs, woodwork, and jewelry, and food vendors hawking a range of traditional Moroccan foods line the streets to cater to the throngs of people shopping at the markets. One of my favorite street foods was kefta—spiced, cigar-shaped meat patties. Here, I use ground lamb and veal and shape them into patties to serve in pita bread with a spicy tomato-cucumber salad.

3 tablespoons olive oil

2 medium Spanish onions, minced

3 garlic cloves, minced

3 serrano chilies, seeds and ribs removed, finely chopped

1 teaspoon ground coriander

1 teaspoon ground cumin

12 ounces ground lamb

12 ounces ground veal

1½ teaspoons garam masala

1 teaspoon dried oregano

1 teaspoon salt

8 pita breads

Tomato-Cucumber Salad (recipe follows)

Heat the olive oil in a large sauté pan over medium-high heat. When the oil begins to shimmer, add the onions, garlic, and chilies and sauté until the onions are softened, about 7 minutes. Stir in the coriander and cumin, and remove from the heat. Let cool.

Combine the lamb, veal, chili-onion mixture, garam masala, oregano, and salt in a large bowl and mix with your hands. Shape the meat into 8 patties, 3 inches in diameter and 1 inch thick.

Heat a large skillet over medium-high heat. Add the patties, in batches if necessary, and sauté for 5 minutes on each side, until deeply browned and cooked through.

To serve, slice the pita breads open halfway. Put 1 tablespoon of the salad in each bread, add a patty, and top with an additional 2 tablespoons salad.

8 SERVINGS

TOMATO-CUCUMBER SALAD

1 large ripe beefsteak tomato, peeled, seeded, and cut into ¼-inch dice

½ cucumber, peeled, seeded, and cut into ¼-inch dice

2 garlic cloves, minced

2 to 3 pickled jalapeño chilies, finely chopped

1½ tablespoons plain yogurt

Juice of 1 lemon

Salt and freshly ground black pepper

Combine the tomatoes, cucumber, garlic, and chilies in a bowl. Gently fold in the yogurt and lemon juice. Just before serving, season with salt and pepper.

VEGETABLE SAMOSAS

The steep, narrow, cobbled streets of the Bo-Kaap, Cape Town's Muslim district, are a picturesque jumble of brightly colored nineteenth-century homes, shops, mosques, and shrines perched on the slopes of Signal Hill overlooking Table Bay. After exploring a neighborhood spice shop we stopped for dinner at Biesmiellah. One of the neighborhood's oldest and best-known restaurants, they served the flakiest, most delicious samosas I've ever tasted, which inspired this recipe.

4 teaspoons ground turmeric
1 teaspoon ground ginger
1 teaspoon ground cinnamon
1½ cups all-purpose flour
2 teaspoons salt
2 tablespoons peanut oil
1 cup water
Juice of 2 lemons
Vegetable Filling (recipe follows)
About 4 cups peanut oil for deep-frying

Toast the turmeric, ginger, and cinnamon in a small sauté pan over high heat until fragrant, 30 to 60 seconds. Remove from the heat and let cool.

Sift together the flour, toasted spices, and salt into a large bowl, and make a well in the center. Pour the oil, water, and lemon juice into the well. Slowly stir the flour into the liquids until all the liquid has been absorbed.

Turn the dough out onto a floured work surface and knead until it is smooth and elastic and begins to form into a ball, about 10 minutes. Transfer to a bowl, cover with a damp cloth or oiled plastic wrap, and let rest in a warm, draft-free place for 20 minutes.

Divide the dough into 12 equal pieces. One at a time, roll out each piece on a floured work surface to a 6-inch circle. Place a generous tablespoon of the filling in the center of each circle of dough. Brush the edges with a little water, and fold the dough over the filling to make a half-moon. Crimp the edges with a fork to seal. Let rest for 30 minutes.

Heat 3 inches of peanut oil in a deep pot to 350°F. Working in batches, carefully add the samosas and fry, stirring occasionally, until golden, about 10 minutes. Remove from the oil with a slotted spoon and drain on paper towels.

Serve with Yogurt Dip (page 43) and Mango Sambal (page 37).

MAKES 12 PASTRIES

VEGETABLE FILLING

2 tablespoons olive oil
1 small yellow onion, sliced
2 small Yukon Gold potatoes (about 8 ounces total), peeled and cut into 2-inch cubes
1 tablespoon curry powder (store bought)
1 carrot, peeled and cut into 2-inch pieces
2 garlic cloves, minced
½ head cauliflower, cut into florets
½ cup coconut milk
½ cup water
Juice of 1 lime

Heat the oil in a large sauté pan, preferably nonstick, over medium heat. Add the onion and potatoes and sauté until the onion is translucent, about 5 minutes. Reduce the heat to low, add the curry powder, carrot, and garlic, and cook, stirring occasionally, for 10 minutes. Add the cauliflower, coconut milk, and water, bring to a simmer, and simmer for 15 minutes. Stir in the lime juice, then transfer to a bowl and set aside to cool.

Mash the filling to a chunky puree with a fork.

VEGETABLES ARE USED TO ADD FLAVOR TO A MEAL, lend it texture, or sometimes even take the place of meat. In a society where meat is an expensive luxury and religious beliefs call for numerous fasting days, they provide an inexpensive way to add flair and variety. Whenever possible, practical cooks find a way to use every part of the plant, serving up the leaves of pumpkin and cassava plants in rich and filling stews and soups. Fruit, both wild and cultivated, is abundant in the warm tropical climate of sub-Saharan Africa, so it is put to use as well: I saw avocados, plantains, tomatoes, mangoes, baobabs, and papayas used in everything from soups, stews, and sauces to salads and sides.

African food has spread all over the world, a fact particularly obvious with vegetables. Just as I noticed a clear musical pattern between West Africa and the Caribbean, I also discerned similarities between the vegetables: for example, callaloo, the national dish of Trinidad and Tobago, clearly derives from West African cooking traditions. The same is true of such soul food classics as Hoppin' John and gumbo, which were created by slaves brought to the American South from West Africa.

The recipes in this chapter stem from very traditional recipes based on what I ate, saw, and heard as I traveled, such as Spicy Okra, to new creations using African food as a starting point, like Mustard Greens and Corn. For the best-tasting results, shop like an African: whenever possible, go to your local farmers' market and buy organic ingredients fresh from the earth.

VEGETABLES

LENTIL STEW

My friend Abbe often goes to Ethiopian restaurants with me because the food is so similar to the dishes he grew up with in Somalia. He tells me that there are a few major differences between the cuisines, one being that lentils are a staple in Somalian cooking. I created this stew for him, which is similar to the satisfying stew of hearty lentils called ful.

To save time, you could skip the step of peeling the shelled fava beans, but peeling off the chewy outer skin of each bean makes for a much more tender bite in the finished dish. To remove the skins, blanch the beans in boiling water for 30 seconds, then plunge them into an ice-water bath. Then simply remove the skins and press out the tender inner bean.

1 cup lentils, soaked in cold water for 2 hours and drained

½ cup olive oil

1 medium red onion, minced

2 garlic cloves, minced

3 tomatoes, roughly chopped, or one 15-ounce can tomatoes, chopped

½ cup peeled fava beans

Juice of 2 lemons

2 teaspoons Berbere (page 8) or chili powder

1 tablespoon chopped parsley

½ teaspoon salt

Combine the lentils with 3 cups water in a large saucepan. Bring to a boil, then reduce the heat and simmer for 20 minutes, or until tender. Drain and set aside.

Heat the olive oil in a large sauté pan. Add the onion and garlic and sauté until the onion is translucent, about 5 minutes. Stir in the tomatoes, lentils, fava beans, lemon juice, berbere, parsley, and salt and heat through.

4 SERVINGS

PLANTAIN-COCONUT STEW

There are so many different religions on the continent, with so many different fasting traditions, that as you travel through Africa chances are that at some point you'll end up someplace where people are abstaining from meat. Although I'm not a vegetarian, I do like to have a meat-free meal every few days. Eating this hearty, filling stew with a little bit of rice or a vegetable mash is my idea of a perfect lunch.

1 medium Spanish onion, roughly chopped

2 red chilies, seeds and ribs removed, finely chopped

1 cup coconut milk

Juice of 2 limes

2 tablespoons white wine vinegar

½ cup peanut oil

5 yellow plantains, peeled, quartered lengthwise, and cut into 1-inch pieces

2 teaspoons chopped cilantro

½ teaspoon ground ginger

½ teaspoon salt

Freshly ground black pepper

Combine the onion, chilies, coconut milk, lime juice, and vinegar in a medium saucepan and bring to a simmer over low heat. Simmer for 10 minutes, then remove from the heat and set aside.

Heat the oil in a large sauté pan over medium heat. Add the plantains and cook for 10 to 15 minutes, turning occasionally, until browned on all sides. Remove the plantains with a slotted spoon and drain on paper towels; blot them to remove excess oil.

Add the plantains, cilantro, and ginger to the coconut liquid and bring to a boil to heat the plantains through. Season with the salt and pepper to taste.

4 TO 6 SERVINGS

TWO-ALARM PUMPKIN CHILI

Dorothy Saucier, a Starbucks barista in South Carolina, grew up in a family of cooks. Her mother made a perfect pie and her brother, a gourmet cook, is an expert at sophisticated menus. Dorothy was inspired by the beauty of Africa in creating her chili recipe.

"When I think of Africa, all the beautiful warm colors of nature come to mind—the browns, oranges, yellows, and rich reds. I wanted to honor that beauty by creating a dish built around native ingredients that incorporate Africa's incredible color palette."

This chili is actually better the second day, after the flavors have had the chance to meld.

1 cup (8 ounces) dried black-eyed peas, picked over

1 12-ounce bottle dark beer

3 tablespoons cooking oil

1 large onion, diced

1 large yellow bell pepper, diced

2 cups fresh or frozen corn

2 hot peppers, such as jalapeño, Scotch bonnet, or habanero, or to taste, seeded and minced

2 pounds pumpkin or butternut squash, peeled, seeded, and cut into ¾-inch cubes (6 cups)

1½ cups water

1 cup strong brewed coffee or espresso

1 6-ounce can tomato paste

2 tablespoons chili powder

1 tablespoon ground cumin

2 teaspoons pumpkin pie spice

1 teaspoon salt

¼ teaspoon sugar

FOR SERVING

Plain yogurt

Toasted pepitas (pumpkin seeds)

Rinse the black-eyed peas. Soak them in the beer for 4 to 6 hours, until they have plumped.

Heat 2 tablespoons of the oil in a large pot over medium-high heat. Sauté the onion and bell pepper until the onion is translucent. Add the corn and sauté for 2 to 3 minutes. Turn up the heat, add the last tablespoon of oil, and stir in the peppers and pumpkin. Cook, stirring, for 2 to 3 minutes, until the cubes start to brown.

Pour the peas and beer into the pot. Add the water, coffee, tomato paste, chili powder, cumin, pumpkin pie spice, salt, and sugar. Bring to a boil, then reduce heat to low, cover, and simmer, stirring occasionally, for 1½ to 2 hours, until the pumpkin and beans are tender.

To serve, ladle into bowls. Garnish each serving with a dollop of yogurt and a liberal sprinkling of pepitas.

SERVES 6 TO 8

BLACK-EYED PEAS

Here in the United States, black-eyed peas are best known as the basis for the Southern rice-and-beans dish Hoppin' John, which is thought to bring luck and prosperity when eaten on New Year's Day. But in fact this bean originated in West Africa, where it is a popular ingredient in any number of dishes. My friend Keke is from Ghana, and his mother told me about one of her favorite dishes, red-red, a stew of fried plantains and boiled black-eyed peas that is common at Ghanian tables. This version of black-eyed peas is made distinctive with coconut milk, ginger, and berbere. It's a great accompaniment to grilled meat or fish.

1 cup black-eyed peas, soaked in cold water for 8 hours and drained

¼ cup Spiced Butter (page 20) or 4 tablespoons (½ stick) unsalted butter

1 medium red onion, sliced

2 tomatoes, chopped

1 Scotch bonnet chili, seeds and ribs removed, finely chopped

2 garlic cloves, chopped

One 1-inch piece ginger, peeled and chopped

2 teaspoons Berbere (page 8) or chili powder

1 cup coconut milk

1 teaspoon ground turmeric

1 cup chicken stock

1 teaspoon salt

2 cilantro sprigs, chopped

1 scallion, trimmed and sliced

Combine the peas with 4 cups water in a large saucepan and simmer, uncovered, for 45 minutes, or until tender. Drain and set aside.

Melt the butter in a deep pot over medium heat. Add the onion, tomatoes, and chili and sauté until the onion is translucent, about 10 minutes. Add the garlic, ginger, berbere, and coconut milk and bring to a simmer. Stir in the turmeric and chicken stock and bring to a simmer, then reduce the heat to low and simmer, uncovered, until the sauce thickens, about 20 minutes.

Add the peas and salt and simmer until most of the liquid is absorbed, about 20 minutes.

Stir in the cilantro and scallion, and serve.

4 TO 6 SERVINGS

DISCOVERY OF A CONTINENT

CANDIED YAMS AND PLANTAINS

egend has it that the word "yam" comes from a misunderstanding between Portuguese slave traders and a group of workers who were digging up the tubers in the area that today is Guinea. When asked what the tubers were called, the Africans answered, "Nyami"—"something to eat" in their language—and the name stuck.

Yams and plantains are two of the staples of West African cooking. In this recipe, I play off the natural sweetness of both for a hearty, filling side dish that's a great complement to slow-cooked meats and game.

2 medium yams (about 2 pounds total), peeled and cut into 6 pieces each

3 tablespoons Spiced Butter (page 20) or unsalted butter, melted

¼ cup soy sauce

1 cup orange juice

¼ cup honey

½ teaspoon ground cumin

½ teaspoon ground ginger

2 medium green plantains, peeled (see page 4) and cut into 3-inch pieces

Preheat the oven to 350°F. Arrange the yams in a baking dish and brush with the butter. Roast for 20 minutes.

While the yams are roasting, combine the soy sauce, orange juice, honey, cumin, and ginger in a small bowl and whisk until well blended.

Add the plantains to the yams and pour ½ cup of the orange juice glaze over the plantains and yams. Return to the oven and roast for another 20 minutes, or until tender, brushing every 5 to 10 minutes with the remaining glaze.

8 SERVINGS

CHUNKY MASHED VEGETABLES

This recipe is inspired by irio, a Kikuyu dish made from mashed greens, potatoes, corn, and beans that is served throughout Kenya, Tanzania, and Uganda. I love pureed vegetables, particularly potatoes, but I personally think when they are too smooth they taste like baby food. This recipe solves that problem by adding chunks of beans, carrots, and onions to mashed sweet potatoes.

6 garlic cloves, peeled

2 sweet potatoes, peeled and cut into 1-inch cubes

½ cup peanut oil

1 pound green beans, ends trimmed and cut into quarters, or frozen green beans

½ cup Spiced Butter (page 20) or 8 tablespoons (1 stick) unsalted butter

One 3-inch piece ginger, peeled and finely chopped

3 medium carrots, peeled and cut into ½-inch dice

1 medium red onion, coarsely chopped

2 jalapeño chilies, seeds and ribs removed, finely chopped

1½ cups water

1 tablespoon Berbere (page 8) or chili powder

1 tablespoon chopped chives

1 teaspoon salt

2 tablespoons olive oil

Preheat the oven to 350°F. Toss the garlic and sweet potatoes with the peanut oil in a roasting pan. Roast for 20 minutes, or until the garlic is tender. Remove and reserve the garlic. Continue roasting the sweet potatoes until tender, about 25 minutes.

While the sweet potatoes are roasting, if using fresh green beans, bring a large pot of salted water to a boil. Prepare an ice bath by filling a large bowl with ice and water. Add the beans to the boiling water and blanch for 2 minutes. Drain the beans and plunge into the ice bath to stop the cooking and set the color. Drain and set aside.

When the sweet potatoes are done, transfer them to a large bowl, add the roasted garlic, and mash with a fork to a chunky consistency.

Melt the butter in a large sauté pan over medium heat. Add the ginger, carrots, onion, and jalapeños and sauté, stirring occasionally, until the onion is translucent, about 10 minutes. Stir in the water and bring to a simmer, then reduce the heat and simmer gently until the carrots are tender, about 10 minutes. (If using frozen green beans, add them with the carrots.)

Stir in the berbere and mashed sweet potatoes, then add the blanched green beans and cook, stirring, until heated through. Stir in the chives and salt and transfer to a serving bowl.

Drizzle the vegetables with the olive oil and serve.

4 TO 6 SERVINGS

CRISPY VEGETABLES

These crispy vegetables make a great party dish. I stack them on a large platter and set them out with an assortment of dips and condiments for people to pick at. A mandoline works best to shave the potato and cassava into paper-thin slices, but if you don't have one, use a vegetable peeler to cut slices as thin as you can. Any root vegetables will work—you can also try parsnips and salsify.

1 baking potato, peeled and cut into thin slices

1 medium cassava root, peeled and cut into thin slices

1 teaspoon ground turmeric

1 teaspoon curry powder

1 teaspoon chili powder

½ cup cornstarch

1 cup all-purpose flour

About 4 cups peanut oil for deep-frying

1 green plantain, peeled (see page 4) and cut into thin slices

2 ripe but firm avocados, pitted, peeled, and cut lengthwise into 8 wedges each

1 cup dried chickpeas, soaked in cold water for 24 hours and drained

1 eggplant, cut into 3 x ½-inch sticks

2 carrots, peeled and cut into 2 x ½-inch sticks

2 medium red onions, thinly sliced into rings

Salt

Put the potato and cassava in a colander and rinse under cold water until the water runs clear, about 25 minutes. Pat dry and set aside.

Toast the turmeric, curry powder, and chili powder in a small sauté pan over high heat until fragrant, about 30 seconds. Remove from the heat, and toss the toasted spices with the cornstarch and flour in a small bowl.

Heat 3 inches of peanut oil in a large deep pot to 350°F. Meanwhile, combine the plantain, avocados, chickpeas, eggplant, carrots, and onions in a large bowl. Add the potato and cassava and toss with the spiced flour. Tap off any excess flour. Working in batches, using a slotted spoon, carefully add the vegetables to the hot oil and fry, turning occasionally, until golden brown and crisp, about 5 minutes. Transfer to paper towels to drain, then sprinkle with salt.

Serve with Mango Sambal (page 37), Chickpea-Eggplant Dip (page 26), and Za'atar (page 23) mixed with olive oil.

8 SERVINGS

Mutton

Sea Food

Lamb

WHEN ONE OF MY FRIENDS WENT TO VISIT RELATIVES IN AFRICA she accompanied her aunt to the market to do the weekly shopping for the twenty or so people who lived in the household. She described running alongside her aunt, delighted with the incredibly high quality and freshness of the mushrooms, tomatoes, plantains, mangoes, and other produce she saw. Although her obvious enthusiasm for everything they shopped for hurt her aunt's bargaining efforts, she went back again and again throughout her visit, because she was so enthralled with the array of fantastic produce for sale.

I thought of her story the first time I visited the Merkato in Addis Ababa. The Merkato is one of the biggest open-air markets in Africa, covering several square miles, and it is truly the heart of the city. It was unlike any market I'd ever seen, with everything from clothes and tires, to butter, coffee and spices, to pots and pans for sale in different areas. But the hub of the Merkato is the produce market, where local farmers bring their fruits and vegetables to sell at one of the thousands of busy stalls.

My first impression was one of utter chaos. People darted everywhere to buy and sell, and there was zero tolerance for onlookers. Work begins before 4:30 A.M., when that day's produce is unloaded and sold to the guys who run the stalls. Once that trading is finished, customers start flocking to the market to buy food for their families, streaming in until late afternoon.

The Merkato is amazing, but it's by no means uncommon. Even the smallest African villages have a tiny vegetable market where local farmers sell their harvest and the locals gather to shop, do business, or just visit. And the markets in many of the larger cities are legendary. Since the end of the fourteenth century, Cairo's Khan al Khalili market has been the city's center of commerce. Today, it's an enticing array of one-stop shopping for everything you need, from household goods and tea to melons, gold and silver jewelry, and bootleg technology. To the west, residents of Marrakech buy vegetables, rugs, shoes, and anything else they could possibly need at colorful souks that made me feel like I'd stepped into another century. Each market I visited throughout the continent was different, but one thing always held true: bargaining was part of the process of shopping, and no shop or stall owner expected to be paid the amount they first gave you. I quickly got into the act and had as much fun bargaining as I did shopping.

Here in the United States, I often hear people say that San Francisco has the best food markets—beautiful, locally grown fruits and vegetables, neatly organized and arranged in spotless markets. But as I look back on the loud, vibrant, spectacular markets I saw in each of the places I visited, my vote goes for the bustling, busy, enchanting markets of Africa.

MUSTARD GREENS AND CORN

Although they are rarely used in many parts of the United States, mustard greens have a spunky, pungent flavor unlike any other greens that I know. When cooked on their own, mustard greens can be a predictable dish, so here corn and okra are added to the spicy greens to intensify their flavor, making the dish a great accompaniment to simple grilled fish or steak.

8 okra pods, cut into 1-inch pieces

6 cups mustard greens, roughly chopped

4 ears corn, shucked

3 tablespoons canola oil

1 medium Spanish onion, finely diced

3 garlic cloves, minced

2 bird's-eye chilies, seeds and ribs removed, finely chopped

One 3-inch piece ginger, peeled and grated

1 teaspoon chili powder

4 tomatoes, peeled and chopped

1 teaspoon mustard seeds

1 teaspoon coriander seeds

2 cups chicken stock

1 teaspoon salt

Bring a large pot of salted water to a boil. Prepare an ice bath by filling a large bowl with ice and water. Add the okra to the boiling water and blanch for 30 seconds, then remove with a skimmer or slotted spoon and set aside. Return the water to a boil, add the mustard greens, and blanch for 30 seconds. Transfer to the ice bath to stop the cooking and set the color. Let cool for a few minutes, then drain and set aside. Add the corn to the boiling water, reduce the heat, and simmer for 10 minutes. Remove, and when cool enough to handle, cut the kernels from the cobs. Set aside.

Heat the oil in a large sauté pan over medium heat. Add the onion, garlic, chilies, and ginger and sauté until the onion is translucent, about 5 minutes. Add the chili powder, tomatoes, mustard seeds, coriander seeds, chicken stock, and the corn and okra. Cover, bring to a simmer, and simmer for 10 minutes.

Fold in the mustard greens and cook until heated through, about 2 minutes. Season with the salt.

8 SERVINGS

ROASTED EGGPLANT AND PLANTAINS

My friend Clare told me that in Uganda plantains are eaten in so many ways that there are dozens of different words to describe them. Her favorite preparation is motoke. One of the staples of the country, it is made by wrapping the peeled fruit in banana leaves and burying the packets in ashes to cook until they are soft and sweet. To serve, the plantains are mashed and served like fufu: people grab a bit of the mash in their hand, roll it into a ball with their fingers, and make an indentation in the center with their thumb to scoop up sauces. The plantains in this recipe are roasted to echo the sweetness of motoke, but I've added eggplant and spices to give them a rounder, more elegant flavor.

4 green plantains (not peeled)

1 medium eggplant

2 tablespoons unsalted butter, melted

½ cup coffee

1½ teaspoons brown sugar

1 teaspoon salt

1 teaspoon ground ginger

½ teaspoon ground cinnamon

½ teaspoon ground cardamom, preferably freshly ground

Pinch of ground nutmeg

½ cup soy sauce

1 tablespoon maple syrup

1 tablespoon chopped chives

Preheat the oven to 375°F. Arrange the whole plantains on a baking sheet and roast until the skin starts to color, about 7 minutes. Remove from the oven and set aside to cool slightly.

Meanwhile, cut the eggplant lengthwise in half and brush the cut sides with the melted butter. Arrange on a baking sheet and roast until tender, 20 to 30 minutes. Remove from the oven and set aside until cool enough to handle, then scoop the eggplant flesh into a blender, add the coffee, and puree until smooth (leave the oven on). Transfer to a serving bowl.

When the plantains are cool enough to handle, peel them and cut into 1-inch pieces. Combine the brown sugar, salt, ginger, cinnamon, cardamom, nutmeg, soy sauce, and maple syrup in a large bowl. Add the plantains and toss to coat. Arrange the plantains on a baking sheet and roast for 5 minutes.

Fold the plantains into the eggplant puree and sprinkle with the chives.

4 TO 6 SERVINGS

FALAFEL WITH QUICK TOMATO SAUCE

Falafel is said to have originated in Egypt, where it is now one of the national dishes. In Egypt it is typically made with dried broad beans but I prefer the nutty taste you get from chickpeas. Because falafel tends to be dry, I like to serve it with a dipping sauce. The flavor-rich tomato sauce that is drizzled over these falafel is a nice change of pace from the tahini sauce that traditionally accompanies it.

1 cup dried chickpeas, soaked in cold water for 24 hours and drained

1 small Spanish onion, quartered

3 garlic cloves, lightly crushed and peeled

1 teaspoon ground coriander

1 tablespoon ground cumin

1 teaspoon chili powder

½ cup chopped parsley

2½ teaspoons salt

½ teaspoon freshly ground black pepper, or to taste

½ teaspoon baking soda

1 tablespoon fresh lemon juice

About 4 cups peanut oil for deep-frying

1 egg , if needed

Combine the chickpeas, onion, garlic, coriander, cumin, chili powder, parsley, salt, pepper, baking soda, and lemon juice in a food processor and pulse until finely chopped but not pureed; scrape down the sides of the bowl as necessary and add 1 to 2 tablespoons water if needed.

Heat 3 inches of oil in a large deep pot over medium-high heat to 350°F (the oil is ready when a pinch of the chickpea mixture begins sizzling immediately when added to it). Working in batches, scoop out heaping tablespoons of the mixture, shape them into balls or small patties, and fry, turning occasionally, until golden brown, 3 to 5 minutes. If the patties are brittle or if the mixture separates in the oil, stir the egg into the mixture and continue frying.

Serve the falafel in pita bread with Tomato Sauce (page 41) and shredded iceberg lettuce.

4 SERVINGS (MAKES 12 TO 16 PATTIES)

SPICY OKRA

People tend to either love or hate okra, which originated in Africa and spread to Arabia, Europe, the Caribbean, Brazil, India, and the United States. I happen to love it and think it adds great texture and color to meals, but I do remember being a little put off by its slimy texture the first time I had it. Once you get over that, it's easy to like. Look for pods that are uniform in color, with no discoloration or soft spots. Smaller pods are usually more tender than large pods.

1½ pounds okra, cut into 1-inch pieces
2 tablespoons peanut oil
2 medium red onions, sliced
4 tomatoes, chopped
2 bird's-eye chilies, seeds and ribs removed, chopped
½ cup peanuts, coarsely chopped
3 garlic cloves, minced
½ teaspoon salt, or to taste

Bring a medium saucepan of salted water to a boil. Add the okra and simmer until tender, about 5 minutes. Drain and pat dry.

Heat the oil in a large sauté pan over high heat. Add the onions, tomatoes, chilies, and peanuts and sauté, stirring frequently, until the onions are translucent, about 5 minutes. Reduce the heat to medium, add the garlic, and cook until golden, about 5 minutes. Stir in the okra and cook until heated through, about 2 minutes. Season with the salt.

4 TO 6 SERVINGS

VEGETABLE TAGINE

No dish typifies the cooking of the Maghreb—Morocco, Algeria, and Tunisia—more than tagines. These sweet and savory stews made of any combination of ingredients are cooked in earthenware pots with a distinctively shaped conical lid and typically served with couscous. This vegetarian version features a hearty mix of vegetables. Since most American kitchens aren't equipped with a tagine, it's made in a large skillet.

2 parsnips, peeled and cut into 1-inch chunks
2 baking potatoes, peeled and cut into 1-inch cubes
2 beets, peeled and cut into 1-inch cubes
½ cup olive oil
2 eggplants (skin on), cut into 2-inch cubes
1 medium Spanish onion, cut into 1-inch chunks
4 garlic cloves, minced
½ cup olives, halved and pitted
2 jalapeño chilies, seeds and ribs removed, finely chopped
2 teaspoons ground turmeric
1 teaspoon ground cumin
2 cups vegetable stock
1½ teaspoons salt, or to taste
2 tablespoons chopped parsley
½ cup raisins

Combine the parsnips, potatoes, and beets in a Dutch oven or other large pot, cover with water, and bring to a boil. Reduce the heat and simmer until tender, about 25 minutes. Drain and set aside.

Heat the olive oil in a large sauté pan over medium heat. Add the eggplants, onion, garlic, olives, and jalapeños and sauté until the eggplants are tender, about 10 minutes. Stir in the turmeric, cumin, stock, and the parsnips, potatoes, and beets, add the salt, and bring to a simmer. Reduce the heat to low and simmer for 20 minutes.

Remove the pan from the heat and stir in the parsley and raisins. Taste and adjust the seasoning before serving.

4 TO 6 SERVINGS

A BEAUTIFUL THING ABOUT TRAVELING through a continent as enormous as Africa is that it never stops surprising you. I knew Africa had a culinary tradition of fish and seafood. Coastal Africa is surrounded by the frigid Atlantic Ocean, the balmy Mediterranean Sea, and the temperate waters of the Indian Ocean, and the interior is dotted throughout with freshwater lakes and rivers. As I traveled through this vast landscape, I had some of the finest fish and seafood I've ever eaten, and the scope of the preparations and the variety were truly inspiring.

Every region I traveled to had its own special seafood traditions—North Africans feast on the sardines that populate the Mediterranean; South Africans love their snoek, a long, bony relative of the barracuda that's unique to their area; in landlocked Ethiopia, river and lake trout are a favorite; in Angola, prawns are simmered in coconut milk with tomatoes, ginger, and chilies and served over mashed coconut meat; and in West Africa, fish and rice are on the menu at every important occasion. In fact, fish and seafood play such a vital role that the African continent is home to the only country I know of that is actually named for the bounties of the sea: the name Cameroon is derived from the Portuguese word for shrimp, "camarão."

I enjoyed so many different fish dishes on my journey that choosing which to include in this chapter was a challenge. The following recipes are just a sampling of the riches of the African seas that I discovered.

FISH AND SEAFOOD

BARBECUED SNAPPER

Barbecue is one of the quintessential cooking techniques you'll find throughout West Africa. To me, true barbecue has a slightly charred flavor, which comes from the caramelization of the sugar in the sauce. To attain this result here, the snapper is cooked over a low heat so the sauce doesn't burn but gets the desirable slightly charred taste. A charcoal grill will give you optimal flavor, but this works just as nicely on a gas grill or—especially for city dwellers like me—even in a grill pan. If using a grill pan, use 6-ounce snapper fillets and grill for 5 minutes on each side. On an outdoor grill, you may prefer to use a nonstick porcelain grill pan or rack and place the fish in a nonstick fish basket to keep it from sticking and breaking up.

One 3-pound snapper, cleaned and scaled
2 lemons, cut in half
½ cup olive oil
1½ cups Barbecue Sauce (page 36)

Make 3 diagonal slashes about ¼ inch deep in each side of the fish. Toss together the lemons and olive oil in a large baking dish and place the fish in the dish, turning it to coat and rubbing some of the oil into the slashes and the cavity. Cover and refrigerate for 4 hours, turning two or three times.

Prepare a medium grill fire. Remove the fish from the marinade and brush generously on both sides with the barbecue sauce. Grill for 10 minutes, brushing frequently with the barbecue sauce. Turn and cook for another 10 minutes, continuing to brush with the sauce. Transfer the fish to a serving platter, tent with foil, and let sit for 10 minutes.

While the fish is resting, bring the remaining sauce to a boil in a small saucepan, then transfer to a small serving bowl.

Serve the snapper with the sauce and Roasted Eggplant and Plantains (page 93).

4 SERVINGS

FRIED CATFISH

work with different fish every day and have developed a mental shorthand that automatically pairs certain fish with specific parts of the globe—for example, salmon makes me think of Sweden, toro makes me think of Japan. Catfish, in my mind, is always associated with the American South. Along with fried chicken, ribs, and grits, it is a quintessential food of the region and just one of the culinary contributions of slaves from West Africa and the Caribbean. This recipe is a tribute to the many great women cooks of the American South who preserve the traditional regional cooking, especially the legendary cook Leah Chase, who took me under her wing and taught me everything I know about the rich culinary legacy of the Southern states.

1 tablespoon peanut oil, plus about 4 cups oil for deep-frying
½ cup Ginger Paste (page 14)
1 pound catfish fillets, cut into 3-inch pieces
1 tablespoon mild chili powder
¼ teaspoon cayenne pepper
2 tablespoons cornstarch
Salt
½ cup all-purpose flour

Mix together the 1 tablespoon peanut oil and the ginger paste. Brush the catfish all over with the paste. Cover and refrigerate for 30 minutes.

Combine the chili powder, cayenne pepper, cornstarch, 1 teaspoon salt, and the flour in a medium bowl. Dredge the fish pieces in the flour mixture, tapping off any excess.

Heat 3 inches of peanut oil to 350°F in a deep pot. Carefully add the fish and fry until golden brown, stirring occasionally, about 5 minutes. Remove the fish with a slotted spoon and drain on paper towels, then sprinkle with salt.

Serve with Chili Mayonnaise (page 32) and Crispy Vegetables (page 89).

4 SERVINGS

DISCOVERY OF A CONTINENT

CHERMOULA-ROASTED BASS

A lot of people like flavorful food but they don't particularly care for spicy food. For these people, chermoula fits the bill—it serves up flavor without spiciness and is rich, floral, and flavorful without being overpoweringly hot, making it a great seasoning for bass or any other firm, white-fleshed fish.

In this recipe, I use two techniques to keep the fish moist. Cooking it on the bone helps to prevent the meat from drying out, while wrapping the fish in banana leaves—a technique that's used throughout West Africa—keeps it moist and intensifies the flavors.

2 tablespoons olive oil
One 3- to 4-pound sea bass, cleaned and scaled
Salt
½ cup Chermoula (page 10)
1 banana leaf (page 1) or about a 4-foot length of parchment paper
1 lemon, thinly sliced
3 garlic cloves, cut in half
1 lemon, quartered, plus lemon wedges for serving

Preheat the oven to 350°F. Brush a baking sheet with the olive oil. Make 3 deep diagonal slashes, all the way to the bone, in each side of the fish. Generously sprinkle salt on each side and in the cavity, then brush both sides of the fish and the cavity with the chermoula.

Lay the banana leaf or a 4-foot length of parchment paper on a work surface, and lay the fish across the leaf, about 2 inches from one short end. Arrange the lemon slices and garlic cloves over the fish. Squeeze the juice from the lemon quarters over it. Fold the end of the banana leaf or parchment over the top of the fish, fold the sides in, then wrap the rest of the leaf or parchment around the fish. Tie the packet around the middle and at the ends with kitchen string. Place on the baking sheet.

Roast for 40 minutes, or until the fish is cooked through. Carefully unwrap the fish to check for doneness; the flesh should be opaque and just flaky.

Transfer to a platter, garnish with Preserved Citrus Peel (page 35), and serve with lemon wedges and garlic.

4 SERVINGS

My most vivid memories of Dakar revolve around the sea.

THE SENEGALESE CAPITAL, DAKAR, is the westernmost point of Africa, sitting on a peninsula that juts into the Atlantic Ocean. Given its location, it's no surprise that the most vivid memories of my visit there revolve around the sea.

My time in Dakar was short, so I was lucky to have two guides—Abdullah, the nephew of a friend from New York, and his twenty-six-year-old aunt, Aminata—to show me around. Knowing I was interested in food, they took me to markets around the city. Late one sunny afternoon we set off for Simbujen, the beachfront fish market where returning fishermen unload and sell their daily catch. It was a magical day that gave me an upfront glimpse into day-to-day life in Dakar.

To get to the market, we walked along the edge of a cliff overlooking the Atlantic Ocean. Vans—so overloaded that the back doors were left open to accommodate more passengers—whizzed past us on the busy street. Down below on Koussoum Beach, swarms of men were exercising, jogging, or doing calisthenics in unison on the sand. "They do this every day before and after work, all year long," Abdullah explained.

A brightly colored fishing boat skimmed along the surface of the Atlantic Ocean to land on the beach as we approached Simbujen. My first sight of the market was a neat row of pirogues—fishing boats, painted in the vivid red, green, and yellow of the Senegalese flag—lined up on the beach. Beyond that I saw row after row of women standing behind trestle tables, hard at work scaling, gutting, and cutting fresh mackerel, sole, snapper, mullet, and eel into chunks. All around them was the bustle of a typical African market; laughing children ran between the stalls and neighbors socialized while young girls walked through the crowd selling bissap—a refreshing sweetened tea brewed from hibiscus blossoms—from trays balanced on their heads.

The market opens when the fishermen haul in their catch, around 5:00 P.M., and lasts until about ten each night. It is where Westernized and traditional Senegal meet: businesswomen in Western-style suits on their way home from the office shop alongside women in traditional dress with heads swathed in colorful scarves. Amid the whirl of activity, one figure in particular caught my attention—an older woman with a commanding presence who sat on a low stool surrounded by a circle of men. After watching their interchanges for a few moments, I realized that she was auctioning off the day's catch to be sold at market the next day. She was truly a woman in charge of the situation, not a sight I saw often in the male-dominated society of Senegal.

Beyond the ocean, Dakar is a most impressive place. It's a city of French influences, I noticed as I strolled through the old town—with its tree-lined avenues, storefront cafés, and terra-cotta rooftops. In the newer parts of the city, however, there was no need to remind myself of where I was—it's unmistakably African. Dakar is a chaotic city of people on the go, and everywhere I went, it seemed like everyone had something to sell. Music was everywhere, and Senegalese music is perhaps the most famous of any on the entire continent. No visit to Dakar is complete without a visit to one of the many downtown clubs—including Thiossane, the nightclub run by the legendary Senegalese singer, songwriter, and composer Youssou N'Dour—where live music is performed nightly.

Like many of the other places I visited in Africa, Dakar struck me as a city that embraced its traditions while moving into the twenty-first century. I've read that it's believed the name Dakar is derived from the Wolof tribe's word for refuge. I can't think of a more apt name for this city of beautiful sights and gracious people.

LOBSTER SKEWERS WITH COUSCOUS-AVOCADO SALAD

thought of lobster as one of the most upscale foods around until I visited the market in Zanzibar, where fresh lobster skewers were sold for a few shillings alongside sugarcane drinks, Zanzibari "pizzas," doughnuts, samosas, and French fries. Sitting at a picnic table with my friends, feasting on the ridiculously inexpensive lobster skewers while a blur of street people, tourists, and Masai vendors swirled around us, was one of my most perfect meals in Africa. This recipe re-creates the spirit of that simple but satisfying meal I enjoyed on the shores of the Indian Ocean while the frantic magic of Zanzibar played out before me.

Four 1½-pound lobsters

1 cup couscous

½ cup olive oil, divided

2 grapefruits, peel and white pith removed, segments cut from membranes

1 teaspoon chili powder

1 tablespoon chopped cilantro, divided

2 teaspoons chopped mint, divided

2 ripe avocados, pitted, peeled, and cut into ½-inch cubes

4 tomatoes, cut into quarters

2 garlic cloves

Grated zest and juice of 2 limes

Salt

Soak 8 bamboo skewers in water for at least 30 minutes. Prepare a hot grill fire.

Fill a lobster pot or large stockpot with salted water and bring to a boil. Working in batches if necessary, add the lobsters and boil for 5 minutes. Remove the lobsters from the water and let cool.

Meanwhile, prepare the couscous according to the package directions. Toss with 2 tablespoons of the olive oil, then add the grapefruit segments, chili powder, half the cilantro, half the mint, and the avocados and toss again.

Remove the meat from the lobster claws and tails and cut into 2-inch pieces. Alternate the lobster and tomatoes on the bamboo skewers. Set aside.

Combine the remaining cilantro and mint, the remaining ¼ cup plus 2 tablespoons olive oil, the garlic, lime zest, lime juice, and salt in a blender and blend until smooth. Brush liberally over each skewer. Place on the grill and cook, turning once, for 3 minutes on each side, or until grill marks appear and the lobster is just cooked through.

Serve with the couscous salad.

4 SERVINGS

SALMON SKEWERS WITH TAMARIND SAUCE

I am always on the lookout for new recipes and ingredients, and everyone I meet becomes a source of information and inspiration. My friend Kingsley's mother was the muse for this recipe: during one of her annual visits to New York, she invited me over for a lavish Saint Lucian feast, including a dish made with tamarind. It reminded me how much I love this tart, lip-puckering fruit, which I use here as a complement to rich and oily salmon.

To ensure that the skewers don't stick, make sure the grill grate is hot first. You'll know the fish is cooked through when the salmon flesh easily releases from the grill without sticking.

½ cup peanut oil

2 pounds salmon fillet, cut into 2-inch cubes

¼ cup olive oil

1 medium yellow onion, roughly chopped

1 garlic clove, minced

1 tablespoon curry powder

1 cup white wine vinegar

¼ cup dry red wine

1 tablespoon cornstarch

2 tablespoons tamarind paste (see page 5)

2 teaspoons sugar

½ teaspoon salt

Pour the peanut oil into a medium bowl, add the salmon, and turn to coat. Set fish aside for 30 minutes. Soak 16 bamboo skewers in water for at least 30 minutes. Prepare a medium-hot grill fire.

While the salmon is sitting in the peanut oil, heat the olive oil in a large sauté pan over medium heat. Add the onion and garlic and sauté until onion is translucent, about 5 minutes. Stir in the curry powder, vinegar, red wine, cornstarch, tamarind paste, and sugar and bring to a simmer. Reduce the heat to low and simmer for 5 minutes, or until the sauce thickens slightly. Remove from the heat and let cool slightly, then transfer to a blender and puree until smooth. Transfer 1 cup to a small serving bowl and set aside. Reserve the remaining sauce for basting the salmon.

Sprinkle the salmon with the salt and thread onto the skewers. Arrange on the grill and cook for 3 to 4 minutes on each side, or just until cooked through, brushing frequently with the tamarind sauce.

Serve with Roti (page 67) and the bowl of reserved sauce.

6 TO 8 SERVINGS

MALATA

The waters that surround Mozambique offer an overwhelming range of fresh seafood, including incredible clams that are the centerpiece of malata, a seafood stew that showcases a number of typical African ingredients: peanuts, pumpkin, pumpkin leaves, and chilies. In Mozambique, this dish would often be made with canned or dried clams, but here I call for fresh clams, which give a wonderful briny taste, and substitute spinach for the hard-to-find pumpkin leaves.

⅓ cup peanut oil

1 cup peanuts

1 pound butternut squash, seeded and cut into 1-inch dice

1 medium Spanish onion, diced

4 garlic cloves, minced

4 bird's-eye chilies, seeds and ribs removed, finely chopped

One 3-inch piece ginger, peeled and minced

4 dozen littleneck clams, scrubbed

½ cup bottled clam juice

½ cup dry white wine

2 teaspoons chopped thyme

½ teaspoon salt

4 cups coarsely chopped spinach

2 limes, quartered

Heat the peanut oil in a large sauté pan over high heat. When the oil shimmers, add the peanuts, butternut squash, onion, and garlic and sauté until the onion is translucent, about 10 minutes. Stir in the chilies and ginger and cook, stirring occasionally, for 10 minutes.

Add the clams, clam juice, white wine, thyme, and salt, cover, and cook until the clams open, about 10 minutes. As the clams open, transfer them to a large bowl. Discard any unopened clams.

Add the spinach to the sauté pan, cover, and cook until the spinach has wilted, 2 to 3 minutes. Return the clams to the pan to warm them through.

Divide the malata among four warmed serving bowls and serve with the lime wedges.

4 SERVINGS

DISCOVERY OF A CONTINENT

SHRIMP PIRI PIRI

P iri piri, the national dish of Mozambique, was one of the first African foods I tried when I was cooking in Europe. After the first bite I could see why it's so popular, not only in Mozambique but also throughout the southern regions of Africa and in Brazilian and Portuguese cooking. In Mozambique, piri piri is typically served with rice to cut the spiciness. I use Bibb lettuce, which takes away some of the heat for a very well-balanced dish.

12 jumbo shrimp, peeled and deveined
½ cup plus 2 tablespoons Piri Piri (page 33), divided
2 tablespoons olive oil
½ teaspoon salt
1 lime, quartered
12 Bibb lettuce leaves

Toss the shrimp with ½ cup of the piri piri in a large bowl. Refrigerate for 20 minutes.

Heat the olive oil in a large sauté pan over medium heat. Add the shrimp and cook for 2 minutes on each side, or until opaque throughout. Transfer to a plate and sprinkle with the salt. Squeeze the lime quarters over the shrimp.

Spread ½ teaspoon of the remaining piri piri sauce on each lettuce leaf. Place a shrimp on each leaf and fold over bottom and sides to form a wrap. Serve immediately.

4 SERVINGS AS AN APPETIZER

COD STEW WITH SESAME SEEDS

met Muna—a woman who was born in Libya, raised in France, and now lives in New York—at an art opening, and she generously shared with me her memories of Libyan food. As Libya is one of the few African countries colonized by Italy, its food is a lot more Italian-influenced than in Morocco and Tunisia, where stews and savory dishes tend to be sweeter. This fish stew takes its flavor reference points from the Italian-based traditions of Libyan cooking, featuring tomatoes, garlic, and za'atar.

1 cup blanched whole almonds

4 garlic cloves, cut in half

1 teaspoon grated ginger

6 tomatoes, roughly chopped, or 3 cups roughly chopped canned tomatoes

2 jalapeño chilies, finely chopped, seeds and ribs removed

2 teaspoons Za'atar (page 23)

4 cups chicken stock

Salt

2 green plantains, peeled (see page 4) and diced

1 cup cooked black beans, rinsed if canned

10 ounces morning glory or spinach

2 pounds cod fillet, cut into 1-inch pieces

2 tablespoons olive oil

1 teaspoon sesame oil (not toasted)

2 tablespoons sesame seeds

Juice of 2 limes, or to taste

Toast the almonds in a large pot over low heat until golden brown and fragrant, about 5 minutes. Add the garlic and ginger and cook, stirring constantly, until aromatic, about 1 minute. Add the tomatoes, jalapeños, za'atar, chicken stock, and 1 teaspoon salt and bring to a simmer over medium-high heat. Reduce the heat and simmer gently for 25 minutes.

Stir in the plantains and simmer for 10 minutes. Stir in the beans, then add the morning glory and cod, and simmer for 5 minutes. Remove from the heat, cover, and let sit until the stew begins to thicken, about 15 minutes.

Meanwhile, heat the olive oil and sesame oil in a small sauté pan over low heat. Add the sesame seeds and sauté, swirling the seeds in the pan, until golden and fragrant, 5 to 7 minutes. Remove from the heat.

Just before serving, gently fold the sesame seeds into the stew, then season with the lime juice and salt to taste.

6 SERVINGS

SPICY TILAPIA STEW

The tilapia-rich rivers that crisscross Zambia provide the people there with an abundant supply of this popular, mellow-flavored fish. It's eaten in many ways, but Suzyo, a Zambian woman I met through a friend, described an unusual preparation that I found intriguing: air-dried tilapia is slow-cooked with tomatoes, onion, mild curry, and vegetables until the bones are soft enough to eat.

This recipe substitutes fresh tilapia for a variation on this traditional stew, but you could also use an equal amount of salmon, snapper, or halibut. You can have the fish market fillet the fish, but ask them to save the bones.

One 2-pound tilapia

2 tablespoons peanut oil

2 medium red onions, sliced

6 garlic cloves, cut in half

3 bird's-eye chilies, seeds and ribs removed, thinly sliced

2 jalapeño chilies, seeds and ribs removed, finely chopped

One 2-inch piece ginger, peeled and grated

1 teaspoon ground cumin

1 teaspoon coriander seeds

1 teaspoon mustard seeds

1½ teaspoons cracked black peppercorns

1 teaspoon salt

1 cup long-grain white rice

4 cups water

4 tomatoes, quartered, or 2 cups roughly chopped canned tomatoes

2 cups shredded Napa cabbage

Juice of 2 limes

1 tablespoon chopped parsley

1 tablespoon chopped cilantro

Fillet the tilapia, discarding the head and reserving the backbone. Cut the fillets into 2-inch pieces. Cut the backbone into 4 pieces.

Heat the oil in a large stockpot or Dutch oven over low heat. When it shimmers, add the onions, garlic, chilies, ginger, cumin, coriander, mustard seeds, peppercorns, salt, and rice and sauté for 2 minutes. Add 3 cups of the water and the fishbones, bring to a simmer, and simmer, uncovered, until the bones rise to the surface, about 10 minutes. Remove the bones and discard.

Add the remaining 1 cup water, the tomatoes, and cabbage, and simmer until the cabbage is wilted, about 3 minutes. Add the fish, remove from the heat, cover, and let sit, stirring occasionally, for 6 to 7 minutes, until the fish is just cooked through.

Stir in the lime juice, parsley, and cilantro and serve.

4 TO 6 SERVINGS

TROUT WITH SPINACH SAUCE

As I made my travel plans for Tanzania, I envisioned romantic images of Masai herdsmen and the jagged peaks of Mount Kilimanjaro. Once I got there, it was much more modern than my imaginings but still wonderful. The capital, Dar es Salaam, is right on the Indian Ocean, and most of the city's action takes place on the beaches, where Arabs, Indians, and black Africans gather for business and for socializing. There, I caught my first glimpse of members of the Masai tribe; dressed in their distinctive red-checked blankets and carrying traditional ball-ended clubs, they stood out on the busy beach. While I was in Dar, I had a delicious stew made of fish and spinach sauce, which I re-create here in a quick and easy version.

1½ pounds trout fillets, cut into 2-inch pieces

½ cup peanut oil, divided

4 garlic cloves, minced, divided

One 2-inch piece ginger, peeled and grated

2 jalapeño chilies, ribs and seeds removed, minced, and divided

Juice of 2 lemons

2 teaspoons chili powder

1 small yellow onion, diced

½ teaspoon salt

1 cup chicken stock

2 cups trimmed spinach leaves

1 to 2 canned hearts of palm, rinsed and cut into 1-inch pieces

1 ripe tomato, roughly chopped

Place the fish in a baking dish or other container large enough to hold it in a single flat layer. Combine 2 tablespoons of the peanut oil, half the garlic, the ginger, half the jalapeños, and the lemon juice and pour over the fish, turning to coat. Sprinkle with the chili powder, turning the pieces to coat evenly. Let marinate in the refrigerator for 20 minutes.

While the trout is marinating, heat 2 tablespoons of the oil in a large deep pot over medium-high heat. Add the onion, the remaining garlic and jalapeño, and the salt and sauté until the onion is translucent, 3 to 5 minutes. Add the chicken stock and spinach, bring to a boil, and boil for 2 to 3 minutes, until the spinach is tender, then transfer to a blender and puree until smooth. Transfer to a large bowl.

Wipe out the pot, return it to medium heat, and add 2 tablespoons oil. When it shimmers, add the hearts of palm and tomato and sauté until the hearts of palm begin to color and the tomato starts releasing its juices, about 2 minutes. Stir into the spinach.

Heat the remaining 2 tablespoons oil in a large sauté pan over high heat. Add the trout and sear for about 2 minutes on each side, until just opaque. Fold into the spinach puree, and serve.

4 SERVINGS

WHEN YOU'RE DEALING WITH A PLACE AS DIVERSE as the African continent, it's rare to come up with generalities that can be applied to the cuisine. But as people from all over Africa told me about the foods of their homeland, whether it was Morocco, Ethiopia, Kenya, Mali, or South Africa, one thing became clear: meal time means it's time for friends and family to gather round the table.

Because people tend to live together in large groups, there is always a large crowd around the table, and stews are an integral part of most countries' cuisines.

Just as they are elsewhere in the world, poultry and meat are typically the centerpiece of a meal. Chicken is an affordable luxury in Africa, and many families raise their own. Because they are allowed to forage, the meat of these chickens is stringy and tough, but home cooks accommodate for this short-coming in the most delicious ways. Stews like Ethiopia's doro wett or Morocco's chicken tagine are slow-cooked for hours to produce tender, succulent, flavorful meat.

Pricier meats are typically dishes of celebration. In the Maghreb, a lamb is roasted, while in Kenya, nyama choma—the national dish, made of grilled goat meat—is served. South Africans grill fine cuts of meat, and a variety of game meats.

As I ate my way through Africa, I realized that there is an essential difference between African cooking and the European and American approach. African cooking is much looser and unstructured. You could never substitute lamb for chicken in fried chicken, for example, but in Africa the meat often serves as the backdrop for the dish, and it's the preparation that is the essential component.

In this chapter, you'll find recipes that give an overview of African meat and poultry dishes, along with updated versions inspired by my travels that combine my favorite African flavors with the tastes that I love. Try one of these recipes anytime you want to bring a taste of Africa to your table.

KENYAN COFFEE BARBECUE PORK TENDERLOIN

Scott Rosenthal, a Starbucks store manager in New Jersey, based this recipe on a meal he and his wife shared on their honeymoon.

"Whenever I think of that meal, I remember our wedding and the experience of starting a life with my wife. This African-inspired dish represents one of the first memorable experiences we shared as a married couple."

Roasting the pork very slowly in a low oven makes it extremely juicy and tender, perfectly complemented by the tangy slaw, lightly sweet fries, and the dark, pungent barbecue sauce.

PORK TENDERLOIN

2 1-pound pork tenderloins
2 cups apple cider
2 tablespoons olive oil
¼ cup tandoori spice
1 tablespoon freshly ground black pepper

KENYAN COFFEE BARBECUE SAUCE

½ cup brewed Kenyan coffee
½ cup ketchup
¼ cup cider vinegar
½ cup molasses
2 garlic cloves, minced
1 small onion, minced
1 ounce (1 square) unsweetened chocolate

SWEET JICAMA SLAW

1 cup grated jicama
1 cup grated carrots
¼ cup chopped walnuts
¼ cup dried cranberries
¼ cup cider vinegar
Salt and freshly ground black pepper

YAM AND PLANTAIN FRIES

2 yams
3 green plantains
8 cups vegetable oil
2 tablespoons ground cinnamon
2 tablespoons sugar
Salt

To make the pork tenderloin: Marinate the tenderloin in the apple cider, refrigerated, for at least 4 hours, turning occasionally.

Preheat the oven to 250°F.

Remove the meat from the cider (reserve ½ cup of the cider) and pat it dry with a paper towel. Rub each tenderloin with half the olive oil, tandoori spice, and pepper. Place in a large ovenproof skillet or a baking pan and pour the ½ cup cider around the meat. Roast until the internal temperature is 155°F, 1 to 1½ hours. Allow the meat to rest for 10 minutes.

To make the barbecue sauce: Combine all the ingredients except the chocolate in a small saucepan and bring to a boil over medium heat, stirring frequently. Reduce the heat and simmer gently for 30 minutes, until the sauce is reduced and thickened. Add the chocolate and cook, stirring often, until the chocolate is melted, 2 to 3 minutes. Set aside until ready to serve.

To make the slaw: Combine the jicama, carrots, walnuts, and cranberries in a bowl. Pour the vinegar over the slaw and toss lightly. Season to taste with salt and pepper and refrigerate until serving time.

About 20 minutes before the pork is cooked, make the fries: Peel the yams and plantains. Using a vegetable slicer or sharp knife, cut into 4-inch-long, ¼-inch-thick fries. Pat dry with a paper towel. Pour the oil into a large, deep, heavy saucepan and heat to 375°F. Add the yams and then the plantains in batches and fry until golden brown, about 3 to 4 per batch. With a slotted spoon, transfer to a paper towel–lined platter to drain, and dust with the cinnamon and sugar. Sprinkle very lightly with salt.

To serve, cut the tenderloin into ½-inch slices and arrange over a mound of the slaw on each plate. Drizzle with some of the barbecue sauce and pile the fries on the side. Pass the remaining sauce.

SERVES 6 TO 8

CHICKEN MOFONGO

I kicked off my exploration of African cooking with a trip to the Bronx Terminal Market in New York City. After prowling the market for an hour and a half checking out smoked fish and meats, spices, pastries, and other African foods, I was so hungry I stopped for lunch at a nearby Puerto Rican diner. I ordered chicken mofongo, a hearty, filling stew of mashed plantains, chicken, and hot sauce that has its roots in the cooking of West Africa. It is the embodiment of the poor man's cooking you see throughout Africa and the Caribbean—filling, nourishing, and inexpensive.

Keep an eye on the cassava as it cooks and remove it from the heat as soon as it is tender; if it overcooks, the texture becomes somewhat gelatinous.

¼ cup fresh lemon juice

2 tablespoons Piri Piri (page 33)

6 boneless chicken thighs, cut crosswise into 2-inch strips

1 medium cassava root, peeled, rinsed, and cut into 2-inch cubes

1 medium sweet potato, peeled and cut into 2-inch cubes

2 tablespoons peanut oil

2 medium red onions, chopped

4 garlic cloves, minced

2 Scotch bonnet chilies, seeds and ribs removed, finely chopped

2 scallions, trimmed and chopped

4 small parsley sprigs, leaves only, chopped

Whisk together the lemon juice and the Piri Piri in a shallow pan. Add the chicken, turning to coat, then cover and refrigerate for 2 hours. Remove the chicken from the liquid and pat dry.

Meanwhile, place the cassava in a bowl and rinse in cold water until the water runs clear. Drain.

When ready to finish the dish, combine the cassava and sweet potato in a pot, cover with salted water, bring to a boil, and boil for 25 minutes, or until tender but not mushy. Drain, then transfer to a large bowl and mash with a fork to a chunky consistency.

While the cassava and sweet potatoes are cooking, heat the peanut oil in a large sauté pan over high heat. Add the onions and chicken strips and sauté for 5 minutes, stirring frequently, until the onions are translucent and the chicken is browned. Add the garlic and chilies and cook for another 10 minutes, or until the chicken is cooked through. Remove the pan from the heat and stir in the scallions and parsley.

Fold the chicken into the cassava–sweet potato mash. Serve warm, with Tomato Sauce (page 41) and Mustard Greens and Corn (page 92).

Note: For a more elegant presentation, pack each serving of mofongo into a lightly oiled ramekin or cup, then unmold onto a serving plate.

4 TO 6 SERVINGS

DISCOVERY OF A CONTINENT

CHICKEN STEW (DORO WETT)

When I take people out for Ethiopian food for the first time, this chicken stew, called doro wett (also spelled doro we't, doro wat, and doro wet), is a great introduction. It's the first Ethiopian dish I ever had, and I immediately liked the tender meat, the spicy eggs, and the flavorful sauce laced with berbere and ginger. It's a great dish to make for people who haven't eaten African food before, because it's easy to understand and like.

Don't be alarmed when the sauce doesn't bind together and thicken like a traditional European-style sauce—it should in fact be liquidy and broken to soak into the injera it is served on.

2 medium red onions, diced

Salt

¼ cup Spiced Butter (page 20) or 4 tablespoons (½ stick) unsalted butter, divided

¼ teaspoon ground cardamom, preferably freshly ground

¼ teaspoon freshly ground black pepper

3 cloves

2 garlic cloves, finely chopped

One 1½-inch piece ginger, peeled and chopped

1 tablespoon Berbere (page 8) or chili powder

2½ cups chicken stock, divided

One 4- to 5-pound chicken, cut into 10 pieces, wings reserved for another use

¼ cup dry red wine

Juice of 1 lime

2 hard-boiled eggs, peeled

Combine the onions, a pinch of salt, and half of the spiced butter in a Dutch oven or other large deep pot over low heat. Cook, stirring occasionally, until the onions are golden, about 15 minutes. Add the remaining butter, the cardamom, black pepper, cloves, garlic, ginger, and berbere and cook until the onions soften and take on the color of the spices, about 10 minutes.

Add 2 cups of the chicken stock and the chicken legs and thighs, bring to a simmer, and simmer for 15 minutes. Add the remaining ½ cup chicken stock and the wine, bring back to a simmer, and simmer for 10 minutes. Add the chicken breasts and simmer for 20 minutes.

Gently stir in the lime juice and eggs and simmer for another 5 minutes. The sauce will be loose and soupy. Season with salt to taste.

6 SERVINGS

A S MY CAB LURCHED THROUGH THE streets of Addis Ababa, I reflected that I never imagined I'd be in a car with a live ram strapped to the top. But here I was, on my way to an Ethiopian cooking lesson, and the ram was a gift to my host. I couldn't have been more excited.

One of the first people I'd met in New York was Yeworkwoha "Workye" Ephrem, the chef-owner of Ghenet, an Ethiopian restaurant in New York City's NoLIta. Workye had arranged for her mother, Muluwork Asfaw, a master of traditional Ethiopian cooking, to give me a cooking lesson. Although she thought it was funny that a man would want to learn to cook—in Ethiopia, the kitchen is still a woman's domain—she was ready to teach me to make doro wett, the chicken stew that is Ethiopia's signature dish. When I arrived, I gave her the ram, which she tethered in the front yard among her chickens, and the lesson began.

I hadn't realized what an undertaking this lesson would be. Ethiopian dishes are made up of ingredients that are intensely flavored—and incredibly labor inten- sive to prepare. Berbere, the flavorful blend of dried chili peppers and spices used in nearly all Ethiopian dishes, takes days to make; instead of plain butter, Ethiopian cooking calls for a homemade spiced butter called nit'ir qibe. It is this layering of flavors that makes Ethiopian cooking so distinctive—and so delicious.

Everything was made from scratch. We started with the live chickens that roamed in the front yard, which we butchered, cleaned, and cured before cook- ing. I later learned just how important a step this was; it is said that before an Ethiopian girl marries, she must know the proper way to butcher a chicken for doro wett. As Mrs. Asfaw instructed me, she worked from memory without a recipe, adding a pinch of this and a dash of

that to the simmering pots. Working side by side in her kitchen I remembered my Swedish grandmother, who taught me how to cook and would beam approval when I did something right, just as Mrs. Asfaw was doing.

Hours later, as the stew was finishing, guests began drifting in and out of the kitchen. Mealtimes are social events in Ethiopia, so nearly a dozen family members and neighbors had been invited to join us when we sat down to eat. The fruits of our daylong labor were arranged on a buffet, and the table was set with bottles of tej (honey wine), talla (the traditional home-brewed beer), and bottles of homemade liqueurs. We ate leisurely as we relaxed around the table. It was a very loving atmosphere—you could sense that every- one cherished Ethiopian culture and the country's past.

And that past is truly amazing. Once known as Abyssinia, Ethiopia is the land of Solomon and the Queen of Sheba. Some of the oldest churches in the world dot the mountainous landscapes, and three of the world's major religions—Judaism, Christianity, and Islam—have coexisted for centuries within Ethiopia's borders, blending to form a culture of tolerance and respect for differences.

Ethiopia is known as the land of thirteen months of sunshine. Most of the country is perched on a mile-high plateau; the rest ranges from a river gorge deeper and wider than the Grand Canyon to towering mountains reaching 15,000 feet above sea level, which kept out foreign invaders until the Italian occupation of 1936. As a result, Ethiopian culture and cuisine is largely undi- luted by foreign influences. Ethiopians cherish this unadulterated way of life—in fact, the way Mrs. Asfaw taught me to prepare our feast is not far removed from the way those same dishes were prepared hundreds of years ago.

123

MOROCCAN-STYLE DUCK BREASTS

When I grew up in Sweden, saffron was a spice we used during the Christmas holidays, particularly in the sweet breads we baked to celebrate the feast of St. Lucia. But this lovely, floral spice is used all along the northern and southern coasts of the Mediterranean, too, often in savory dishes. I especially like saffron as a complement to the rich and gamey meat of duck, particularly when it's paired with typical Moroccan spices. I suggest using a hen, which isn't as flavorful as the male drake but is much more tender. Scoring the breasts results in better absorption of the marinade and easier rendering of the excess fat during cooking. Leaving the duck uncovered in the refrigerator will result in a crisper skin, so plan ahead for best results.

3 cups orange juice

2 teaspoons Ras al-Hanout (page 20)

2 cloves

1 cinnamon stick

4 saffron threads

4 white cardamom pods

2 parsley sprigs, chopped

2 garlic cloves, minced, divided

2 medium red onions, diced, divided

One 3-inch piece ginger, peeled and minced, divided

Four 8-ounce boneless duck breasts

Salt

½ cup roughly chopped unsalted cashews

Bring the orange juice to a boil in a medium saucepan. Add the ras al-hanout, cloves, cinnamon stick, saffron, and cardamom and boil for 3 minutes. Add the parsley, half the garlic, half the onions, and half the ginger. Remove from the heat and let cool.

Score the skin of the duck breasts in a diamond pattern. Transfer the duck to a deep tray or baking dish. Pour the orange juice mixture over the breasts and refrigerate, uncovered, for about 2 hours.

Remove the duck breasts from the marinade and pat dry with a paper towel; reserve the marinade. Season the duck with salt. Heat a sauté pan large enough to accommodate the breasts without crowding. Add the breasts, skin side down, and cook over high heat until the skin is crisp and deeply browned, about 6 minutes. Reduce the heat to medium, turn the breasts, and cook until lightly browned and medium rare, about 4 minutes; if you prefer duck cooked to medium, cook for 6 minutes. Transfer to a platter, reserving the fat in the pan, and let rest for 5 minutes.

While the duck breasts are resting, discard all but 2 tablespoons of fat from the pan, and heat the remaining fat over medium heat. Add the remaining garlic, onions, and ginger, and the cashews and sauté, stirring frequently, until the onions are softened, about 4 minutes. Strain the reserved marinade into the pan, turn the heat to high, and simmer until the sauce reduces and thickens, about 5 minutes. Season with salt.

Slice the duck breasts on the diagonal, and serve with the sauce on the side and Vegetable Tagine (page 97).

4 SERVINGS

ROASTED TURKEY LEGS

While European-style cooking usually relies on salt for flavor, African cooks look to spice blends to season poultry, meats, and fish. Featuring a deliciously subtle blend of citrus, spices, and ginger, these turkey legs are a sampler of some of my favorite African flavors prepared with European and American techniques and ingredients. First the turkey legs are rubbed with a spice mix, then they are cooked slowly in oil and butter—very much like a confit—to produce a richly flavored meat that's so tender it almost melts in your mouth.

3 tablespoons salt

4 cups orange juice

4 boneless turkey legs (about 1 pound each)

3 tablespoons Chermoula (page 10)

4 thyme sprigs, chopped

1 cup peanut oil, divided

1 cup Spiced Butter (page 20) or ½ pound (2 sticks) unsalted butter

One 3-inch piece ginger, peeled and grated

Combine the salt with 2 cups of the orange juice in a large bowl and stir to dissolve the salt. Add the turkey legs, cover, and refrigerate for at least 2 hours, but not more than 8.

Drain the turkey and pat dry. Combine the spice mix and thyme and rub generously over and under the turkey skin.

Heat 2 tablespoons of the peanut oil in a Dutch oven or other deep pot over medium heat. Add the turkey legs, in batches if necessary, and sear on all sides for about 4 minutes on each side. Reduce the heat to very low (return all the turkey to the pot), add the remaining 2 cups orange juice, the remaining ¾ cup plus 2 tablespoons oil, the butter, and ginger, and bring to a simmer. Simmer for 1½ hours, stirring occasionally.

Remove the turkey legs from the liquid with a slotted spoon (discard the liquid), and cut the legs in half. Serve with Preserved Citrus Peel (page 35).

6 TO 8 SERVINGS

HARISSA-ROASTED TURKEY BREAST

Every year, my mother served turkey for Christmas, even though I always begged her to make goose instead because I thought turkey was too dry and bland. This recipe puts an end to all my objections to turkey—it's roasted with harissa, the fiery chili sauce that's a staple on every Tunisian table, so it's full of flavor, and it stays deliciously moist with crispy, crackling skin.

One 6-pound bone-in turkey breast (skin on)
Salt and freshly ground black pepper
4 garlic cloves
2 cinnamon sticks
½ medium yellow onion, finely chopped
1 cup Harissa (page 16)
Stuffing (recipe follows)

Preheat the oven to 400°F. Rinse the turkey under cold water and pat dry. Sprinkle on all sides with salt and pepper. Stuff the garlic cloves, cinnamon sticks, and onion into the neck cavity, and seal it closed with a wooden skewer or toothpick. Generously rub the harissa over and under the skin.

Place the turkey breast skin side up on a roasting rack in a roasting pan and cover with foil. Roast, basting occasionally with the juices that accumulate in the bottom of the pan, until an instant-read thermometer inserted into the thickest part of the breast reads 160°F and the juices run clear, about 1½ hours. During the last 20 minutes of cooking, remove the foil to brown the skin. Let the turkey rest for at least 20 minutes before carving.

Serve with the stuffing and Beet-Ginger Chutney (page 29).

6 TO 8 SERVINGS

STUFFING

¼ cup olive oil, divided
2 tablespoons lightly crushed almonds
½ loaf white bread, cut into 1-inch cubes (about 4 cups)
2 medium parsnips, peeled and cut into 1-inch cubes
2 cinnamon sticks
3 garlic cloves, cut in half
3 shallots, cut into ¼-inch dice
2 quinces, peeled, cored, and cut into 1-inch cubes
1 tablespoon Harissa (page 16)
1 cup chicken stock
½ cup orange juice
1 tablespoon honey
2 teaspoons chopped thyme
1 teaspoon salt
½ cup raisins
1 tablespoon chopped parsley

Heat 2 tablespoons of the olive oil in a large sauté pan over medium heat. Add the almonds and bread cubes and sauté for 5 minutes, or until golden brown. Remove from the heat and set aside.

Heat the remaining 2 tablespoons olive oil in a Dutch oven or other large pot. Add the parsnips and cinnamon sticks and sauté for about 5 minutes. Add the garlic, shallots, quinces, and harissa and sauté until the garlic is golden, about 5 minutes. Stir in the chicken stock, orange juice, and honey, reduce the heat to low, and simmer for 15 minutes.

Add the thyme, salt, raisins, and almonds and bread cubes and stir until well combined. Cook over low heat, stirring frequently, until heated through. Stir in the chopped parsley.

DISCOVERY OF A CONTINENT

JERK CHICKEN

have friends from all over the world and when we get together we often have a potluck meal, with everyone bringing a favorite dish from home. My Jamaican friend Donnovan always brings a mean jerk chicken, which is so spicy sometimes you can't eat more than a bite. I toned down the heat in this version, but it still has a really great well-balanced spicing that is characteristic of jerk dishes.

One 3- to 4-pound chicken

½ cup Jerk Mix (page 17)

2 thyme sprigs, cut in half

½ head garlic, top third cut off and papery skin removed

2 Yukon Gold potatoes, peeled and cut into 1-inch cubes

1 sweet potato, peeled and cut into 1-inch cubes

1 medium parsnip, peeled and cut into 1-inch cubes

½ medium Spanish onion, cut into 1-inch cubes

1 pear, peeled, cored, and cut into 1-inch cubes

1 quince, peeled, cored, and cut into 1-inch cubes

Preheat the oven to 350°F. Using your hand, gently loosen the skin of the chicken breast. Generously rub half of the jerk mix under and all over the breast skin. Stuff half the thyme under the skin. Put the garlic in the cavity of the chicken. Truss the chicken. Set aside on a plate.

Combine the Yukon Gold potatoes, sweet potato, and parsnip in a large pot and add enough salted water to cover. Bring to a boil over high heat and boil for about 10 minutes, until just slightly tender. Drain.

Toss the potatoes, sweet potato, parsnip, and onion with the remaining jerk mix, then spread the vegetables in a single layer in a roasting pan. Add the remaining thyme. Place the chicken on a roasting rack above the vegetables, and roast for 45 minutes.

Add the pear and quince to the roasting pan, increase the oven temperature to 375°F, and roast for an additional 30 to 40 minutes, until an instant-read thermometer inserted in the thigh registers 160°F and the juices run clear.

Serve with Yogurt Dip (page 43).

8 SERVINGS

LEMON-OLIVE CHICKEN

One of my most vivid culinary memories is from the start of my cooking career, when I was a cook on a luxury cruise ship that traveled all over the world, stopping at local ports of call to buy fresh ingredients for that night's dinner. The market at Marrakech was my introduction to northern Africa, and to me, this dazzling market with its colorful, abundant displays of food, spices, clothing, and virtually anything else you can imagine is symbolic of Morocco and the rest of the region. Centuries ago, Marrakech became the trading mecca for spices, where European, African, and Middle Eastern merchants met to barter and exchange their wares. This ancient crossroads is still the scene of an exciting mix of cultures, with a highly specialized cuisine that reflects the region's magical past. The bright flavors of lemons, briny olives, and delicate spices are the tastes I associate with Morocco. Combining sour and salty with a balance of spices, this simple roast chicken brings me back to that long-ago day in the market of Marrakech.

One 4- to 5-pound chicken

Salt

10 green olives

5 black olives

4 garlic cloves, peeled

1 tablespoon grated lemon zest

2 shallots, roughly chopped

One 3-inch piece ginger, peeled and cut into three 1-inch pieces

2 tablespoons olive oil

Juice of 2 lemons

1 tablespoon Ras al-Hanout (page 20)

Preheat the oven to 400°F. Generously rub the body and neck cavities of the chicken with salt and sprinkle the skin with salt. Mix together the olives, garlic, lemon zest, shallots, and ginger and stuff into the body and neck cavities. Combine the olive oil, lemon juice, and Ras al-Hanout in a small bowl, and rub all over the breast and legs. Truss the chicken.

Place the chicken on a rack in a roasting pan. Roast until an instant-read thermometer inserted in the thickest part of the thigh registers 160°F, about 60 to 70 minutes.

Transfer the chicken to a platter and let rest for 10 to 15 minutes before carving. Serve with Red Rice (page 59).

4 SERVINGS

HARISSA BEEF SKEWERS

My friend Clare comes from the Ankole kingdom in southern Uganda, where the people are known for their herds of exquisite big-horned cattle. There, beef is the meat of choice, in some cases to the exclusion of anything else: her grandmother, she told me, would only eat beef, and if a piece of fish so much as touched one of the pans in her kitchen, she would throw the pan away.

If you are a city dweller like me and don't have a grill, you can make these beef skewers by arranging the skewers in a single layer on a baking sheet and roasting for 20 minutes in a 425°F oven.

2 cups peanut oil

Juice of 4 lemons

1½ tablespoons Harissa (page 16)

4 sprigs rosemary, leaves only, finely chopped

Six 6-ounce rib-eye steaks, cut into 2-inch cubes

2 green bell peppers, cored, seeds and ribs removed, and cut into 2-inch squares

2 red bell peppers, cored, seeds and ribs removed, and cut into 2-inch squares

4 medium Spanish onions, cut into quarters

4 tomatoes, cut into 6 wedges each

6 scallions, trimmed and cut into 2-inch pieces

1 head Thyme-Roasted Garlic (page 40)

Whisk together the oil, lemon juice, Harissa, and rosemary in a small bowl. Combine the beef, peppers, onions, tomatoes, and scallions in a large zipper-lock bag. Add half the boharat mixture and seal the bag, forcing out the excess air. Marinate in the refrigerator for 2 hours, turning the bag several times. Set the remaining marinade aside.

Prepare a hot grill fire. If using wooden skewers, soak in water for 30 minutes.

Squeeze the roasted garlic cloves into the reserved marinade and mix well. Set aside.

Drain the meat and vegetables, and thread onto metal or wooden skewers, alternating the meat and vegetables.

Grill for 5 minutes on each side, brushing frequently with the reserved marinade. Transfer to a platter and let rest for 5 minutes.

Serve with Spicy Plantain Chips (page 60).

6 SERVINGS

KOFTA MEATBALLS WITH OKRA TOMATO SAUCE

Swedes tend to think that we invented meatballs. But as I learned about food and traveled around the world, I found that it's hard to find where one culture starts and another one ends, because people everywhere have adapted their dishes to make the most of their food supply. In North Africa, meatballs are known as kofta, and are often stuffed with nuts, cheese, or eggs and served in a rich sauce. These rich meatballs combine the flavors of northern Africa with the spicy notes you find south of the Sahara. They are served with tomato sauce, which is commonly used in place of a meat gravy.

3 slices white bread, cut into 1-inch squares
¾ cup milk
½ teaspoon chili powder
½ teaspoon ground coriander
1 pound ground lamb
1 pound ground beef
1 teaspoon salt
2 jalepeño chilies, seeds and ribs removed, finely chopped
3 garlic cloves, minced
2 sprigs parsley, minced
1 tablespoon olive oil
Okra Tomato Sauce (recipe follows)

Place the bread in a small bowl. Pour the milk over the bread, tossing to moisten the bread, and let soak until well softened, about 10 minutes.

Toast the chili powder and coriander in a small sauté pan over high heat until fragrant, 30 to 60 seconds. Remove from the heat.

Combine the lamb, beef, toasted spices, salt, bread, jalapeños, garlic, and parsley in a large bowl and mix with your hands. After wetting hands to prevent sticking, form the mixture into 2-inch balls.

Heat the olive oil in a large sauté pan over medium-high heat. Working in batches, add the meatballs and brown for 4 minutes on each side. Drain on paper towels.

Transfer the meatballs to a large saucepan. Add the tomato sauce and bring to a simmer, then reduce the heat and simmer gently, stirring frequently, until heated through, about 15 minutes.

6 SERVINGS

OKRA TOMATO SAUCE

1½ pounds okra, trimmed
2 tablespoons olive oil
2 medium red onions, chopped
6 tomatoes, diced, or 3 cups chopped canned tomatoes
2 garlic cloves, minced
1 teaspoon ground coriander
1 teaspoon ground cumin
2 cups tomato juice
Juice of 1 lime
Salt

Bring a large pot of water to a boil, add the okra, and boil until just tender, about 6 minutes. Drain and let cool, then cut into ½-inch slices.

Heat the oil in a medium sauté pan over medium heat. Add the onions and sauté until translucent, about 10 minutes. Add the tomatoes, garlic, coriander, and cumin and cook until the garlic is softened, 8 to 10 minutes.

Add the tomato juice, bring to a simmer, and simmer for 10 minutes. Add the lime juice and okra and stir well. Season with salt.

136

DISCOVERY OF A CONTINENT

BARBECUED PORK RIBS

The West African tradition of cooking outdoors over stones was carried to the American South, forming the basis of the most beloved of Southern traditions: barbecue. I love the passion that Southern barbecue inspires—each region thinks its version is the best, whether it's the simple vinegar sauce of the Carolinas, the sweet tomato sauce of Tennessee, or the liquid fire of Texas-style barbecue. Unquestionably, my favorite meat for barbecue is pork ribs, which melt in your mouth when barbecued just right. If possible, use a charcoal grill, which will give you the smoky flavor of authentic barbecue.

2 tablespoons Berbere (page 8) or chili powder

1 cup coffee

½ teaspoon ground ginger

1 teaspoon ground cumin

½ cup packed brown sugar

¼ cup salt

3 racks baby back pork ribs (about 4 pounds)

2 tablespoons olive oil

1 medium red onion, finely chopped

2 garlic cloves, chopped

One 2-inch piece ginger, peeled and chopped

3 tomatoes, quartered, or 1½ cups chopped canned tomatoes

1 small carrot, peeled and chopped

2 tablespoons honey

½ cup water

2 tablespoons red wine vinegar

1½ teaspoons Worcestershire sauce

1 serrano chili, seeds and ribs removed, finely chopped

Combine the berbere, ½ cup coffee, ground ginger, cumin, brown sugar, and salt in a small bowl. Place the ribs in a large baking pan or on a baking sheet and generously rub the berbere mixture over them. Cover and refrigerate for at least 8 hours, or overnight.

Preheat the oven to 325°F. Heat the olive oil in a large, flameproof roasting pan over medium heat. Add the onion, garlic, chopped ginger, tomatoes, and carrot and sauté until the onion is tender, about 10 minutes. Stir in the honey, ½ cup coffee, water, vinegar, Worcestershire sauce, and chili.

Remove from the heat and add the ribs. Cover the pan with a lid or foil and transfer to the oven. Cook for about 2½ hours, turning the ribs every 30 minutes, until the meat has shrunk away from the ends of the rib bones and easily pulls away from the bones. Transfer the ribs to a platter, and set the roasting pan aside.

Meanwhile, prepare a medium-hot grill fire. Grill the ribs on both sides until browned but not charred, 4 to 6 minutes per side. Place on a serving platter.

Skim as much fat as possible from the sauce, and transfer to a serving bowl. Serve the ribs with the sauce, Warm Eggplant–Butternut Squash Salad (page 56), and Corn Bread (page 64).

4 TO 6 SERVINGS

RACK OF LAMB

came up with this recipe for a dinner I was making at the Sheraton Addis Ababa in 1999, during my first visit to Ethiopia. The berbere is incredibly distinctive, giving the tender lamb an assertive, brash flavor. It was one of my first dishes to incorporate Ethiopian ingredients and flavors, and it reflects my personal philosophy as a chef: take classic flavors and add a dash of something unexpected—in this case, the potent spice blend with traditional rack of lamb.

½ cup olive oil

1½ tablespoons coarsely chopped rosemary

1 large garlic clove, smashed

2 frenched racks of lamb (1½ pounds each)

1 tablespoon roasted coffee beans, ground

1 teaspoon salt

½ teaspoon cardamom powder

½ teaspoon chili powder

2 teaspoons Dijon mustard

2 teaspoons beaten egg yolk

¼ cup fine bread crumbs

2 to 3 tablespoons dry red wine, divided

2 tablespoons Berbere (page 8)

½ cup chicken stock

2 tablespoons cold unsalted butter, cut into pieces

Combine the oil, rosemary, and garlic in a large zipper-lock bag. Add the lamb, then seal the bag, forcing out the excess air. Marinate in the refrigerator for 8 to 24 hours, turning the bag several times.

Preheat the oven to 400°F. Make the spice paste: Stir together the coffee, salt, cardamom, chili powder, mustard, yolk, and bread crumbs in a small bowl, then add 1 to 2 tablespoons of the wine, just enough to make a paste. Refrigerate until ready to use.

Remove the lamb from the marinade and pat dry; discard the marinade. Heat a dry, large, heavy sauté pan over high heat until very hot. Reduce the heat to medium-high and brown the lamb, one rack at a time, about 3 minutes per side. Transfer, fat side up, to a large roasting pan.

Smear the spice paste on the fat side of the lamb. Roast until an instant-read thermometer inserted into the center of the rack reads 125°F, for medium-rare, about 18 to 20 minutes. Transfer the lamb to a cutting board and let rest for 10 minutes.

While the lamb is roasting, toast the two tablespoons berbere in a small heavy saucepan over low heat, stirring constantly, until very fragrant, about 1 minute. Add the chicken stock and 1 tablespoon wine and bring to a boil, then boil until reduced to the consistency of a sauce. Remove from the heat and whisk in the butter bit by bit until incorporated.

Cut the lamb into chops and serve the sauce on the side. Serve with Chunky Mashed Vegetables (page 88).

6 TO 8 SERVINGS

VISITED KHAYELITSHA, A BLACK TOWNSHIP on the outskirts of Cape Town, on Freedom Day 2004. As South Africans marked ten years of democratic government, my friends and I joined in the celebration at Vicky's B&B, a four-room shack made of corrugated iron, tree trunks, and wood that is one of the best-known hotels in South Africa. It is run by Vicky Ntozini, an industrious woman with a cheerful smile who gives her guests a taste of township life. As we sat in her living room listening to stories of life in Khayelitsha, Vicky explained the significance of the colors of the South African flag, representing one nation made up of many colors: red, symbolizing the blood of the apartheid years, white for the European settlers, gold for the mineral wealth of South Africa's mines, green for the country's prosperous farming, blue for the two oceans that border the coasts, and black for the black and colored communities that dominate the country's population. She then suggested we experience Khayelitsha ourselves with a visit to the local barbecue joint, and her husband, Piksteel, offered to show us the way. Before setting off, we stopped at the local shebeen (saloon) to pick up a loaf of bread and drinks, because, as Vicky explained, at the market we would find only one thing on the menu: grilled meat.

The main road in Khayelitsha is Amandla Street, named for Nelson Mandela's rallying cry during the anti-apartheid movement. "Amandla" means "power" in the Xhosa language, and even though the dirt road was lined with rows of shacks cobbled together from pieces of corrugated steel and powered with electricity pirated from the overhead electric lines, Amandla Street filled me with hope, because the people I met there were so optimistic and supportive of the way their country is going. In just ten short years, the country has transformed itself from one of the most unjust places on earth into a functioning democracy where everyone has a voice.

As we walked through the streets, passing barbers, beauty salons, and all the other little shops that make up a town's life, a band of children gathered, excited by the novelty of having someone new in town. We formed a sort of parade moving down the dusty road. Along the way, we met the residents of Khayelitsha, many of whom had moved to the townships from the rural areas over the past decade to find work. I think it was this direct tie to rural places that gave these people such balance—although South Africa's big cities are just as modern and developed as, say, New York, if you go a little distance out you are in a completely remote place. While most people I know in the United States and Europe get their peace and balance by going to a spa, or a museum, or the movies, the people I met in Khayelitsha found theirs just by stepping outside.

As we rounded the corner near the market, we passed a man standing behind a table stacked with cow heads. Called smileys because of the way the cow's lips curl over the teeth, cow heads are a special-occasion dish in the townships, where no scrap of meat is wasted. The market itself was run by two women: one who stood behind the counter, selling the meat and brushing away flies, and the other who grilled the meat for you. I chose my piece of meat at the counter, then carried it over to the grill, where it was cooked until thoroughly charred. Sitting on a bench at one of the tables, I feasted on the meat with Piksteel and his friends, wrapping the tough, blackened meat in slices of bread, and for a brief hour was part of the community that defines the South African townships.

BOBOTIE

O n Sunday afternoons, South African families gather for dinner with their families. Whether they are Afrikaners, Cape Malay, or of black descent, there is one dish that can be found on almost all tables throughout the country—bobotie, a one-dish casserole. Like any national dish, the recipe changes from family to family. Malay families might add almonds or raisins, for example, while Afrikaners prepare a simpler version, similar to Britain's shepherd's pie. I serve a Malay-style version at one of my restaurants, and people who try it love the comforting appeal of this hearty home-style dish.

1¼ pounds ground beef

1 medium red onion, finely chopped

2 garlic cloves, minced

1 tablespoon Green Masala (page 15) or curry powder

½ teaspoon ground cumin

½ teaspoon crushed coriander seeds

2 tomatoes, chopped, or 1 cup chopped canned tomatoes

¼ cup bread crumbs

¼ cup crushed peanuts or smooth peanut butter, preferably unsweetened

2 teaspoons salt, divided

1 cup milk

2 large eggs

2 egg yolks

Pinch of ground nutmeg

Heat a Dutch oven or other large heavy pot over medium-high heat. Add the beef and onion and cook, stirring to break up any lumps, until the beef is well browned, about 5 minutes. Stir in the garlic, masala, cumin, coriander, and tomatoes, reduce the heat to low, and cook, stirring occasionally, for 10 minutes.

Stir in the bread crumbs, peanuts, 1½ teaspoons of the salt, and ½ cup water and cook for another 15 minutes, stirring occasionally. Remove the beef mixture from the pot with a slotted spoon and drain on paper towels. Transfer to a plate and refrigerate for 20 minutes.

Preheat the oven to 350°F. Generously butter a 2-quart baking dish. Spread the beef mixture in the bottom of the pan and press down to pack well. Whisk together the milk, eggs, egg yolks, nutmeg, and the remaining ½ teaspoon salt and pour over the beef mixture.

Set the baking dish in a larger baking pan and add enough hot water to the large pan to come 1 inch up the sides of the baking dish. Cover with aluminum foil and bake for 25 minutes. Remove the foil and bake for another 20 minutes, until the custard topping is golden brown and a toothpick inserted in the center comes out clean.

Cut into squares and serve with Mango Sambal (page 37) and Chunky Mashed Vegetables (page 88).

6 SERVINGS

LAMB STIR-FRY

S tir-fry is thought of as an Asian-style food, but Africa has its stir-fries too, particularly sukuma wiki, one of the national dishes of Kenya. There, the focus would be on the greens—usually collard greens, with a little bit of beef or goat meat for flavor—but I've adapted it to showcase lamb and kale. To get the beautifully seared meat of a perfect stir-fry, you need intensely high heat and a pan with a big surface area so that the heat can penetrate the meat quickly. A wok or cast-iron skillet can help you get the high heat you need, but if you don't have one you can make do with a large heavy skillet.

2 tablespoons peanut oil

1 medium red onion, sliced

½ teaspoon ground cardamom, preferably freshly ground

½ teaspoon ground cumin

2 garlic cloves, minced

One 2-inch piece ginger, peeled and grated

8 ounces kale, cleaned and shredded

1½ pounds boneless lamb loin, cut into ½-inch-thick slices

½ teaspoon salt

4 tomatoes, chopped, or 2 cups chopped canned tomatoes

Freshly ground black pepper

Heat the oil in a wok or large heavy skillet over high heat. Add the onion, cardamom, cumin, garlic, and ginger and sauté until the onion is translucent, about 3 minutes. Add the kale and sauté until wilted, about 4 minutes. Remove from the pan with tongs and set aside.

Add the lamb to the hot pan and stir-fry until browned on all sides. Sprinkle with the salt, add the tomatoes, and simmer for 5 minutes.

Return the kale mixture to the pan and stir until heated through, 3 to 5 minutes. Season with pepper and remove from the heat.

Serve with Chunky Mashed Vegetables (page 88).

4 TO 6 SERVINGS

DISCOVERY OF A CONTINENT

MERGUEZ SAUSAGE

Although you can find merguez sausages in Europe and the United States, I associate them with Ramadan because many of the Muslim staff members at Aquavit bring it in to break their fast during the monthlong religious celebration. Unlike many other sausages, which are made with pork, merguez sausages originated in North Africa, where they are made with lamb or beef to comply with Islamic law and spiced with fiery harissa, which gives them heat and a beautiful red color. In this version, I've simplified the process by making merguez without the traditional sausage casing.

1 teaspoon ground cumin

1 teaspoon ground coriander

1 teaspoon cayenne pepper

2 pounds ground lamb

8 ounces ground dark chicken meat

4 garlic cloves, minced

2 teaspoons Harissa (page 16)

2 teaspoons salt

1½ tablespoons chopped parsley

1 tablespoon chopped mint

½ cup olive oil

Toast the cumin, coriander, and cayenne in a small sauté pan until aromatic, about 30 seconds. Remove from the heat and let cool.

Combine the toasted spices, lamb, chicken, garlic, harissa, salt, parsley, and mint in a large bowl and mix well with your hands. Cover and refrigerate for 1 hour to allow the flavors to blend.

Preheat the oven to 350°F. Using wet hands, to keep the mixture from sticking, shape the lamb mixture into golf-ball-sized balls. You should have about 24 balls.

Heat the oil in a large skillet over medium-high heat. Add the meatballs, in batches if necessary, and brown on all sides, turning frequently, about 8 minutes. Remove from the pan and drain on paper towels.

Arrange the meatballs on a baking sheet and bake for 10 minutes, or until cooked through.

Serve with Tomato Sauce (page 41) and Lentil Stew (page 82).

4 TO 6 SERVINGS

STIR-FRIED BEEF STEW

One thing that sets the Ethiopian restaurant scene apart from any place else I've seen is the prevalence of restaurants that serve only one dish. Throughout Addis Ababa, you pass shacks serving nothing but doro wett, shiro, or tibs wett, a traditional Ethiopian-style stir-fry made with beef or lamb. Rich with buttery flavor, tibs wett is one of the easiest Ethiopian dishes to make. It's more like a stir-fry than a traditional stew, cooked in minutes and served immediately so that the tomatoes and jalapeños still taste fresh, not stewed. If you don't have a large wok or a frying pan big enough to accommodate all the meat, cook it in two batches. Traditionally in Ethiopia, this would be served with injera and collard greens, but I also like to serve it with noodles or mashed potatoes.

¼ cup Spiced Butter (page 20) or 4 tablespoons (½ stick) unsalted butter

1 cup thinly sliced red onions

1½ pounds hanger steak or beef tenderloin, cut into ½-inch cubes

1 teaspoon salt, or to taste

1½ tablespoons Berbere (page 8) or chili powder

½ teaspoon ground cardamom, preferably freshly ground

½ teaspoon ground ginger

¼ teaspoon ground cumin

⅛ teaspoon ground cloves

¼ teaspoon freshly ground black pepper

3 garlic cloves, cut into quarters

3 tomatoes, chopped, or 1½ cups roughly chopped canned tomatoes

2 jalapeño chilies, seeds and ribs removed, thinly sliced

½ cup dry red wine

Melt the spiced butter in a wok or large skillet over high heat. Add the onions and cook, stirring constantly, until they begin to color around the edges, about 2 minutes. Add the meat, sprinkle with the salt, and stir-fry until browned on all sides, about 3 minutes on each side.

Stir in the berbere, cardamom, ginger, cumin, cloves, pepper, and garlic. Tilt the pan away from you to avoid the steam that will rise, and carefully add the tomatoes, jalapeños, and wine. Simmer for 1 minute, then season with salt if necessary.

Serve immediately.

6 TO 8 SERVINGS

CHICKEN-PEANUT STEW

A restaurant kitchen can be a virtual United Nations, with a staff made up of people from around the world. A dishwasher at Aquavit who comes from Mali told me about the typical midday meal he had growing up: peanut stew made with onion, tomatoes, and spinach served over rice. His description was the starting point for this peanutty stew, an elegant interpretation of a dish eaten throughout West Africa every day.

2 medium white onions, sliced

2 carrots, peeled and cut into 1-inch pieces

2 Scotch bonnet chilies, cut in half, seeds and ribs removed

One 3-inch piece ginger, peeled and sliced

2 bay leaves

6 white peppercorns

4 cups water

4 boneless, skinless chicken thighs, each cut into 4 pieces

4 boneless, skinless chicken breasts, each cut into 4 pieces

2 cups unsalted peanuts

3 tablespoons olive oil

2 baking potatoes, peeled and cut into 2-inch cubes

4 tomatoes, cut into quarters, or 2 cups roughly chopped canned tomatoes

1 teaspoon salt

1 pound spinach, tough stems removed, washed

Combine the onions, carrots, chilies, ginger, bay leaves, peppercorns, and water in a medium pot and bring to a boil over high heat. Reduce the heat to medium, add the chicken thighs, and simmer, uncovered, for 15 minutes. Add the chicken breasts and simmer for another 10 minutes, or until the chicken is cooked through.

While the chicken is simmering, toast the peanuts in a small dry sauté pan over medium heat until golden brown and fragrant. Let cool, then grind 1 cup of the toasted peanuts in a blender to a smooth paste. Set aside.

Using tongs, remove the chicken from the cooking liquid and set aside. Using a slotted spoon, transfer the vegetables to a food processor; discard the bay leaves. Puree the vegetables until smooth. Set the broth aside.

Heat the oil in a large sauté pan over medium heat. When it begins to shimmer, add the potatoes and sauté until they are golden brown, about 10 minutes. Add the chicken pieces and brown them on all sides, about 10 minutes. Remove the pan from the heat.

Stir the vegetable puree into the broth and bring to a boil. Add the peanut paste and the remaining cup of whole peanuts and whisk until well combined. Add the tomatoes, chicken, and potatoes and simmer until heated through, about 5 minutes. Remove from the heat and season with the salt. Add the spinach and stir until the spinach is wilted.

Serve with Pomegranate Rice (page 57).

4 SERVINGS

ROASTED VEAL SHANKS WITH APRICOTS AND ALMONDS

The floral, fragrant flavors of apricots and almonds complement roasted veal in this special-occasion dish from Morocco that's served at weddings and to honored guests. In the traditional version, dried apricots are soaked overnight before being added to the sauce. This version, using fresh and dried apricots, is less time-consuming but just as special. Whole veal shanks, even if you can find them, are very large and probably too big for most home cooks' pots. Your butcher or grocer will probably stock veal shanks in large slices, which is ideal for this recipe.

8 slices veal shank, ½ inch thick

½ cup Harissa (page 16)

3 tablespoons olive oil

2 medium Spanish onions, sliced

2 cups dry white wine

6 ripe apricots, sliced

Juice of 2 lemons

6 dried apricots, chopped

4 cloves garlic, minced

2 cups chopped blanched almonds

2 cups couscous

4 tarragon sprigs, leaves only

Preheat the oven to 250°F. Rub the veal shanks on top with the harissa until well coated. Arrange the veal in a roasting pan in a single layer, cover, and roast for 2 hours.

Remove 1 cup of the cooking liquid from the roasting pan and set aside. Increase the heat to 350°F and roast until the shanks are tender, about another 30 minutes.

Meanwhile, heat the olive oil in a large pot over medium heat. Add the onions and cook, stirring frequently, until translucent, 5 to 7 minutes. Add the wine, fresh apricots, lemon juice, and the reserved cooking juices, bring to a simmer, and simmer for 30 minutes. Stir in the dried apricots, garlic, and almonds and simmer for another 15 minutes.

While the apricots are cooking, cook the couscous according to the package directions. Set aside.

Add the couscous and tarragon to the apricots and stir to heat through.

To serve, heap the couscous on a large serving platter and arrange the veal shanks around it.

8 SERVINGS

TEA-ROASTED VEAL

Cooking with tea gives meats an earthy flavor. I have long been a fan of using tea when cooking, and when I first tried rooibos, the herbal red bush tea that is a favorite in South Africa, I immediately thought this delicately fragrant liquid would be excellent for curing meats. Rooibos is starting to become available in the United States, but if you can't find red tea at your local market, substitute black tea.

¼ cup salt

2 cups water

½ cup red wine vinegar

1 rosemary sprig, leaves only, minced

¼ cup honey

One 3-inch piece ginger, peeled and chopped

¼ cup red tea leaves or the leaves from 3 tea bags

½ vanilla bean

One 2-pound boneless veal shoulder roast

2 tablespoons Chermoula (page 10)

Combine the salt, water, and vinegar in a saucepan and bring to a boil. Add the rosemary, honey, ginger, and tea leaves. With a sharp paring knife, cut the vanilla bean lengthwise in half, and use the back of the knife to scrape the seeds into the pan. Add the vanilla bean. Bring back to a boil, then reduce the heat and simmer for 5 minutes. Remove from the heat and let cool.

Place the veal in a baking dish. Reserve ½ cup of the tea mixture, and pour the rest over the veal. Cover and refrigerate for at least 8 hours, or overnight, turning occasionally.

Preheat the oven to 325°F. Remove the veal from the tea mixture and pat dry. Smear the roast with the chermoula, and place the veal on a rack in a roasting pan.

Roast the veal for 1 to 1½ hours, basting often with the reserved tea marinade, until an instant-read thermometer inserted into the thickest part of the roast registers 130°F. Tent with foil and let rest for 20 minutes before serving.

Serve with Warm Eggplant–Butternut Squash Salad (page 56).

4 SERVINGS

WHEN I WAS A YOUNG CHEF IN SWEDEN AND FRANCE, a meal followed a prescribed course: appetizer, entrée, dessert. But as I quickly learned when I began to travel outside of Europe, dessert in the way that I knew it is a Western phenomenon. In all the warm climates, the end of most meals is marked with fresh fruit like pineapple slices, orange wedges, mango chunks, or bananas sprinkled with a little sugar or honey. It's a refreshing and healthy way to end a meal, and on a hot and humid day or after a heavy meal, far preferable to a creamy rich cake or pudding. Now I find myself planning my meals the African way: if I want to make a heavy, rich dessert, I'll serve a lighter meal, like a salad and shrimp piri piri, and when I'm making a heavy main course, I'll bring the meal to a close with an orange or a few cookies.

I did discover two distinctly different regions with a strong dessert tradition. In South Africa, where the Dutch culinary influences remain strong, there is an incredibly diverse range of cakes and pastries that are part of the national culinary tradition. I was also fascinated by the distinctive desserts of Morocco that have a purely Arabic sensibility, with pastries doused in honey or sprinkled with orange water, not dusted with powdered sugar or drizzled with sauce, as I was used to seeing.

All of the recipes in this chapter are inspired by the spirit of Africa—they feature flavors that I discovered or grew to appreciate in my travels.

DESSERTS AND DRINKS

ALMOND COOKIES

Almonds play a big part in Moroccan cooking, making an appearance in both sweet and savory dishes. They are the basis for qa'b el-ghazal (horns of the doe), a crescent-shaped pastry with an almond and sugar filling that is almost always served with sweetened mint tea to visitors in Moroccan homes. This cookie is a variation of that traditional pastry that is much less time-consuming to make, but just as delicious. If you can't find almond flour, process 1 cup sliced blanched almonds into a powder in a food processor.

1¾ cups all-purpose flour
1½ cups almond flour
½ teaspoon salt
½ pound (2 sticks) unsalted butter, at room temperature
½ cup sugar
About 1½ cups blanched whole almonds

Sift the flour, almond flour, and salt into a bowl; set aside.

With an electric mixer, cream the butter and sugar in a large bowl. Add the flour mixture and beat until combined. Turn the dough out onto a lightly floured surface and knead for 1 to 2 minutes, until the dough forms a ball. Wrap in plastic and refrigerate for 15 minutes.

Preheat the oven to 325°F. Line two baking sheets with parchment paper or grease them with butter. Shape the dough into 1-inch balls and arrange on the baking sheets, leaving about 2 inches between the cookies. Press an almond into the center of each cookie, flattening it slightly.

Bake for 10 to 15 minutes, until golden. Remove from the baking sheets and cool on a wire rack.

MAKES ABOUT 5 DOZEN COOKIES

MALVA PUDDING

first had this deliciously sticky, cakey steamed pudding at Eziko's, a cooking school and restaurant in the Cape Town township of Langa that serves a menu of traditional South African foods. It's a favorite throughout South Africa, and with good reason—it's homey and comforting, with familiar flavors that are easy to enjoy.

1 cup all-purpose flour

1 teaspoon baking soda

Pinch of salt

1¼ cups sugar, divided

1 egg

1 tablespoon unsalted butter, at room temperature, plus 8 tablespoons (1 stick) unsalted butter

¼ cup apricot jelly

1 cup milk

1 teaspoon white vinegar

1 teaspoon vanilla extract

1 cup evaporated milk

Whipped cream (optional)

Preheat the oven to 350°F. Sift together the flour, baking soda, and salt; set aside.

Beat together 1 cup of the sugar, the egg, the 1 tablespoon butter, and the jelly in a large bowl until pale and fluffy. Beat in the flour mixture.

Butter an 8-inch cake pan; set aside. Mix together the milk, vinegar, and vanilla in a small bowl, then fold into the egg mixture until thoroughly mixed. Pour into the buttered baking dish, and cover with lightly oiled foil.

Bake the pudding for about 30 minutes, until set. The cake will look spongy, with little holes dotting the top.

While the pudding is baking, combine the evaporated milk, the remaining 8 tablespoons butter, and the remaining ¼ cup sugar in a saucepan and heat, stirring, until the butter melts and the sugar has dissolved. Remove from the heat.

Pour the warm sauce slowly over the hot pudding and allow to stand for 10 minutes, or until all the liquid is absorbed. Serve warm with whipped cream.

4 SERVINGS

I WAS IN PAARL, A QUAINT SMALL CITY in the Cape Winelands an hour or so northeast of Cape Town, and my itinerary included a stay at a bed-and-breakfast and dinner at some of the area's finest restaurants. How I got from there to a tiny kitchen in Cape Town's District Six is one of those happy accidents that makes travel such an adventure.

One Saturday night during my stay in Paarl, I was eating dinner and sampling South African wines at Marc's Mediterranean Cuisine—a delightful restaurant owned by the gracious and charming Marc Friedrich—when I noticed a man dining by himself. Earlier in the day, I'd seen him at the inn, so I invited him to join my friends and me at our table. His name was Owen Juilles and, as luck would have it, he was the chef for South African Airlines. He volunteered to show us around Cape Town and introduce us to the food of his heritage: Cape Malay, the beautiful blend of Malaysian, Indian, African, and European cooking that is perhaps the most celebrated cuisine in Africa.

The Cape Malays descended from Indonesians, Sri Lankans, Indians, and Malaysians who were captured and enslaved in the seventeenth and eighteenth centuries by the Dutch East India Company and brought to Cape Town. These slaves created a hybrid cuisine, melding the curries, the chilies, and the spices such as ginger, cinnamon, and turmeric from their homelands with the dull, less flavorful cooking of their Dutch masters. I'd read about the Cape Malay magic for years, and was eager to see and taste firsthand its signature combinations of meat cooked with fruit and the marriage of sweet and savory flavors with hints of spice, curry, and other seasonings.

Owen enthusiastically recounted the Cape Malay dishes I had to try. But most important of all, he said, were koesisters, the traditional doughnutlike pastry served with coffee in all Cape Malay homes every Sunday morning.

The next morning, we set off for the neighborhood where Owen had grown up, District Six, the formerly vibrant Malay neighborhood that was once known as the soul of Cape Town. According to Owen, authentic koesisters could not be found at a bakery but must be purchased from a Cape Malay woman who made them in her home. So we set off through the remains of District Six in search of the real thing.

A girl we passed on the street pointed us to a house where koesisters were sold. Entering the front door, we descended a flight of dark stairs into a narrow house. At the back was a small kitchen, where Gadijah Carim makes and sells doughnuts every Sunday. A petite, soft-spoken Muslim, she shyly told us that she makes a thousand koesisters every week.

She was happy to demonstrate how she cooked the spiced dough in hot oil, then boiled the pastries in simple syrup before dusting them with coconut flakes. During our visit, a stream of people came to her front door, each bringing a container that she filled with koesisters to be taken home and eaten after church.

During my stay in Cape Town, I tried the other Cape Malay specialties Owen urged me to sample, and of all the foods I tried in Africa, Cape Malay became my favorite. But for me, the defining experience of Cape Malay cuisine was eating those steaming hot, freshly baked koesisters, made by hand in Gadijah Carim's tiny kitchen.

CHOCOLATE RUM CAKE WITH CINNAMON WHIPPED CREAM

n Ethiopia there is no cultural tradition of dessert, but all the pastry shops sell beautiful frosted cakes. The grandest of all of them is chocolate cake—rich, dense, and satisfying. It's always served at celebrations and is the perfect gift for a special someone. This cake was inspired by those cakes I saw in the Addis Ababa shops. It also is a tribute to the spice farm I visited in Zanzibar, where I tasted freshly harvested "true" cinnamon—also known as canela—for the first time. More complex and fragrant than the cassia cinnamon you find in most American supermarkets, it had an incredibly intense, pungent aroma unlike any cinnamon I'd ever had before. I've never seen it in stores, but you can get it through mail order sources. Here I pair it with some of my favorite dessert flavorings: chocolate, coffee, and rum. If desired, you can freeze one of the layers to serve later.

4 ounces semisweet chocolate, roughly chopped
¾ pound (3 sticks) unsalted butter, cut into small pieces
¼ cup strong brewed coffee
¼ cup dark rum
2 cups sugar
3 large eggs
2 cups all-purpose flour
1 teaspoon ground cinnamon
⅛ teaspoon ground cloves
1 teaspoon baking powder
½ teaspoon baking soda
½ cup buttermilk
1 teaspoon vanilla extract
Cinnamon Whipped Cream (recipe follows)

Preheat the oven to 350°F. Butter and flour two 8-inch round cake pans, and set aside.

Combine the chocolate and butter in the top of a double boiler or a heatproof bowl set over gently simmering water, and stir frequently until melted. Remove from the heat. Stir in the coffee, rum, and sugar and stir until the sugar is dissolved.

Transfer to a large bowl and beat in the eggs, then stir in the flour, cinnamon, cloves, baking powder, and baking soda. Add the buttermilk and vanilla and mix until well combined and slightly thickened.

Pour the batter into the prepared pans. Bake until a toothpick or cake tester inserted in the center comes out clean, about 30 minutes. Remove from the oven and let cool in the pans on a wire rack for about 20 minutes.

Remove the cakes from the pans and let cool. Slice and serve with the whipped cream.

16 SERVINGS

CINNAMON WHIPPED CREAM

1 teaspoon ground cinnamon
1 cup heavy cream
¼ cup confectioners' sugar
1 teaspoon vanilla extract
2 tablespoons dark rum

Toast the cinnamon in a small sauté pan over medium heat until fragrant, 30 to 60 seconds. Remove from the heat and let cool.

Combine the cream, sugar, and vanilla in a large bowl and beat to semi-stiff peaks. Fold in the cinnamon and rum.

DISCOVERY OF A CONTINENT

GINGER-BANANA SALAD WITH HONEY ICE CREAM

The Bible refers to Ethiopia as the land of milk and honey, and to this day honey still plays an important part in the country's culinary repertoire: tej—the country's national drink—is a sweet wine made from honey, honey breads are commonly served, and Ethiopia is the world's tenth largest honey producer. The sweet, creamy ice cream in this recipe is inspired by the Ethiopian fondness for honey, and provides a silken contrast to the accompanying fruit salad.

½ cup packed brown sugar
One 1-inch piece ginger, peeled and thinly sliced
1 cinnamon stick
¾ cup water
Juice of 1 lemon
½ cup fresh orange juice
4 ripe bananas
Honey Ice Cream (recipe follows)

Combine the sugar, ginger, cinnamon stick, and water in a small saucepan and bring to a boil over high heat, stirring to dissolve the sugar. Remove from the heat and strain into a large bowl. Add the lemon juice and orange juice and chill for at least 1 hour.

Just before serving, slice the bananas on the diagonal into 1-inch pieces. Add them to the ginger syrup, turning to coat them well.

Serve the bananas with scoops of the ice cream, drizzling some ginger syrup over each serving.

6 SERVINGS

HONEY ICE CREAM

4 large egg yolks
¼ cup sugar, divided
1 cup heavy cream
1½ cups milk
⅓ cup honey

Whisk together the egg yolks and 2 tablespoons of the sugar in a small bowl until pale yellow and thick, about 5 minutes.

Combine the cream, milk, and the remaining 2 tablespoons sugar in a large saucepan and bring to a boil over medium heat, stirring to dissolve the sugar. Remove from the heat.

Whisking constantly, slowly add 1 cup of the hot milk mixture to the egg yolks (tempering the egg yolks this way keeps them from curdling or scrambling). Pour the egg mixture into the hot liquid and stir constantly over low heat until the custard coats the back of the spoon, about 5 minutes; do not allow to boil.

Meanwhile, fill a large bowl with ice water; set this ice bath aside.

Remove the custard from the heat and immediately strain it into a medium metal bowl. Nestle it in the ice bath and stir in the honey. Stir frequently until the custard is cool, then refrigerate for at least 2 hours.

Transfer the chilled custard to an ice cream maker and freeze according to the manufacturer's instructions. The ice cream will be soft and creamy. For a firmer consistency, transfer the ice cream to an airtight container and place in the freezer for at least 2 hours; remove from the freezer about 15 minutes before serving.

MAKES ABOUT 1 QUART

KOESISTERS

Cape Towners are justly proud of their koesisters, a doughnut that's a traditional after-church treat on Sundays. My search for the perfect koesister took me to the home of Peter and Marilyn Carelon, an energetic South African couple who run a printing business and a bed-and-breakfast from their home. They had two kinds of koesisters to share—a sweet, braided crullerlike pastry and a dark, round, spiced doughnut. Another version made without spices and dipped in a sugary syrup, known as koeksisters, is typically served in the homes of Afrikaners, but I was particularly fond of the spiced version, which featured notes of cinnamon, ginger, and cardamom.

6 tablespoons warm water

3 tablespoons granulated sugar

1 package active dry yeast (2¼ teaspoons)

2 cups all-purpose flour

1 teaspoon salt

3 extra-large egg yolks

5 tablespoons milk

2 tablespoons unsalted butter

¼ cup packed brown sugar

2 teaspoons ground cinnamon

1 teaspoon ground ginger

1 teaspoon ground cardamom, preferably freshly ground

About 4 cups canola oil for deep-frying

Combine the water, granulated sugar, and yeast in a large bowl and set in a warm place until the yeast begins to bubble, 5 to 10 minutes.

Add the flour and salt to the yeast and mix with an electric mixer on low speed until well combined. Beat in the egg yolks one at a time, beating after each addition until well incorporated.

Combine the milk and butter in a small saucepan and heat until butter is melted. With the mixer running, slowly pour the milk-butter mixture into the dough, beating until combined. Cover with a damp cloth or plastic wrap and let sit in a warm place until the dough doubles in size, about 40 minutes.

Punch the dough down and turn out onto a floured surface. Cut into 20 pieces, roll each one into a ball, and arrange in a single layer on a baking sheet. Set in a warm place and let rise for 20 minutes.

While the dough is rising, toss together the brown sugar, cinnamon, ginger, and cardamom in a large shallow bowl. Set aside.

Heat 3 inches of canola oil in a deep pot to 350°F. Working in batches, add the dough balls and fry, turning occasionally, until golden on all sides, about 3 to 4 minutes. Remove from the oil and drain on paper towels.

Toss the doughnuts in the mixed spices to coat. Serve warm.

MAKES 20 DOUGHNUTS

COCONUT, YAM, AND BANANA FRITTERS WITH A TRIO OF DIPPING SAUCES

K ristin Pearson, a Starbucks barista in Massachusetts, was inspired to create this recipe after a vacation to St. Thomas where she had the pleasure of staying with a college friend and her family. They had lived on the island for a few years after moving from Africa.

"My memories of that trip are tied to food, whether it was the different restaurants we explored each day, or the unique home-cooked dishes that married the flavors of the island with her family's African roots. From conch fritters, to fried plantains, to exotic fruits grown in the backyard, the foods her mother served were unlike any I have tried in America. One evening we enjoyed a tender lamb stew with tropical spiced rice, accompanied by fresh-squeezed passion fruit juice—a dish that reflected their heritage while incorporating locally grown fruits and vegetables. The next morning, we were awoken by roosters crowing and the sound of her father chopping down coconuts. For breakfast, we sipped on fresh coconut water and snacked on hand-picked bananas. This amazing cultural experience was the inspiration for my recipe, which showcases fresh, exotic flavor combinations and the traditional cooking methods of Africa."

Prepare the dipping sauces—one, two, or all three—in advance, so you can enjoy the fritters warm.

COCONUT, YAM, AND BANANA FRITTERS

1 16-ounce can yams in light syrup, drained

2 very ripe medium bananas

3 large eggs

½ cup sugar

2 cups all-purpose flour

1½ teaspoons baking powder

¼ teaspoon salt

½ teaspoon ground cinnamon

¾ cup whole milk

¾ cup sweetened flaked coconut

8 cups vegetable oil

Choice of dipping sauces (see facing page)

Mash the yams and bananas with a fork in a small bowl. Set aside.

In a large bowl, whisk the eggs and sugar until frothy and lightened in color. Scrape down the bowl with a rubber spatula. Sift the flour, baking powder, salt, and cinnamon together. Add half the sifted flour, then half the milk, to the egg mixture. Stir in the remaining flour and milk. Add the mashed yam and bananas and the coconut, stirring just until incorporated.

In a large heavy saucepan, heat the oil to 350°F. Working in batches, drop tablespoons of the batter into the oil. (To keep the oil at the right temperature, do not fry too many at a time.) Fry the fritters, turning occasionally with a slotted spoon, until golden brown on each side, 2 to 3 minutes total. Remove to a paper towel–lined plate to drain. Serve warm with any or all of the dipping sauces.

MAKES ABOUT 6 DOZEN SMALL FRITTERS

COCONUT CREAM SAUCE

½ cup unsweetened coconut milk
¼ cup sugar
2 tablespoons heavy cream

Combine all the ingredients in a small saucepan and heat over medium heat, stirring, until the sugar is dissolved. Let cool to room temperature before serving.

ARABIAN MOCHA SANANI AND CHOCOLATE SAUCE

½ cup hot brewed Arabian Mocha Sanani coffee
¼ cup heavy cream
6 ounces semisweet chocolate, finely chopped, or
1 cup semisweet chocolate chips

Combine the coffee and cream in a small saucepan and bring just to a boil. Remove from the heat and stir in the chocolate. Let stand for about 30 seconds, then whisk gently until the chocolate is melted. Allow to cool slightly; the sauce will thicken as it stands.

SWEET AND SPICY CARAMEL SAUCE

1 cup caramels (about 20), unwrapped
2 tablespoons butter
¼ cup heavy cream
½ teaspoon ground cinnamon
¼ teaspoon ground nutmeg

Melt the caramels and butter together in a small saucepan over low heat, stirring frequently. Add the heavy cream and spices and stir until combined. Serve warm.

TANGERINE CONSOMMÉ WITH TAPIOCA

Most Americans would say they've never tasted cassava, a staple vegetable of West African cooking. But if you've ever eaten tapioca, you've had this ubiquitous root vegetable. Tapioca is derived from cassava, and I like to use it to add a pearly texture to desserts like panna cottas or fruit soups. The first time you have tapioca, the texture can be surprising—but it's a taste that's easy to acquire because it's so interesting. It doesn't have much flavor on its own, so you have to cook it with a flavorful liquid; here I use coconut milk to give the tapioca pearls a rich, full taste, and mix it with some of my favorite fruits. You can use whatever fresh fruits are in season—I call for my favorites, mango, papaya, and raspberries—but you can experiment with passion fruit, blueberries, or the fruits you like best in this refreshing dessert, which plays off the African tradition of ending a meal with fruit.

1 vanilla bean

1 cup sugar, divided

2 lemongrass stalks, sliced

Grated zest and juice of 2 lemons

1 cup water

½ cup small pearl tapioca, soaked overnight in 3 cups water

One 15-ounce can coconut milk

1 cup diced mango

1 cup diced papaya

½ cup raspberries

6 mint leaves, finely shredded

2 cups fresh tangerine juice

With a sharp knife, split the vanilla bean lengthwise, then use the back of the knife to scrape out the seeds. Combine the vanilla seeds, ½ cup of the sugar, the lemongrass, lemon zest, and water in a small saucepan and bring to a boil over high heat. Remove from the heat and let cool, then refrigerate for 30 minutes, or until chilled.

Combine the tapioca and any remaining liquid, the coconut milk, and the remaining ½ cup sugar in a saucepan and bring to a boil. Reduce the heat to low and simmer for 10 minutes, or until the tapioca pearls are tender and translucent. Remove from the heat and let cool.

Stir the mango, papaya, and raspberries into the tapioca and fold in the mint. Set aside.

Strain the chilled lemon syrup into a bowl. Stir in the tangerine juice and lemon juice.

To serve, divide the tapioca among six shallow soup bowls, and pour the consommé around the tapioca.

6 SERVINGS

PINEAPPLE-CASHEW SALAD

n tropical Africa, fresh fruits abound—pineapples, mangoes, oranges, mangosteens, bananas, passion fruit, and countless weird and wonderful fruits I'd never seen or heard of before. To me, fresh fruit is the perfect light, naturally sweet end to a meal. When you're looking for a way to cap off a barbecue or cookout, try this simple fruit salad, which combines pineapple chunks with cashews for a great texture that's dressed up with a dash of white wine and fresh mint.

½ cup sweet white wine, such as Riesling or ice wine

¼ cup packed brown sugar

½ golden pineapple, peeled, cored, and diced (about 1½ cups)

½ cup roasted cashews

4 mint leaves, finely shredded

Pour the wine into a medium bowl and add the sugar, stirring until it is dissolved. Add the pineapple cubes. Cover and refrigerate for 2 hours.

To serve, stir the cashews into the pineapple. Divide among serving bowls and sprinkle with the mint.

6 SERVINGS

MINT ICED TEA

n Morocco, guests are greeted with a steaming cup of green tea flavored with mint and lots and lots of sugar. Traditionally it is served hot, but chilled it makes a refreshing and thirst-quenching beverage that's perfect with a hot and spicy meal.

4 cups water

2 tablespoons sugar

2 tablespoons honey

6 mint sprigs

One 3-inch piece ginger, peeled and sliced

4 teaspoons green tea leaves

1 lemon, cut into quarters

Combine the water, sugar, honey, mint sprigs, and ginger in a large saucepan and bring to a boil, then reduce the heat and simmer for 5 minutes. Add the green tea and simmer for another 3 minutes. Strain and let cool.

Serve the tea over ice cubes, garnished with the lemon.

4 SERVINGS

LEMONGRASS TISANE

This rejuvenating infusion is made with lemongrass, a popular flavoring in sub-Saharan Africa. Hot teas and tisanes—they are rarely served iced—are popular all over the continent, usually served with copious amounts of milk and sugar.

6 cups water
2 stalks lemongrass, coarsely chopped
Milk and sugar for serving

Bring the water to a boil in a medium saucepan. Add the lemongrass, remove from the heat, cover, and let steep for 15 minutes.

Strain the tisane through a fine-mesh sieve, and pour into teacups. Serve with milk and sugar.

6 SERVINGS

SOURCES

Whenever possible, I adapted the recipes in this book to substitute easier-to-find ingredients for African spices, meats, vegetables, and other foods. But in some cases, nothing but the original will do. Most large cities in North America have at least one African market where you can find all sorts of interesting and wonderful ingredients, like sumac, morning glory, dried fish and meats, and ready-to-make fufu or ugali. You can also check out Asian, Caribbean, Latin, Indian, and Middle Eastern markets, which carry a variety of spices and vegetables you can't find at traditional grocery stores. And don't overlook local African restaurants; often the proprietor will be willing to sell regular customers the ingredients they need. For those really hard-to-find items, the Internet is a great resource; I've listed a few of my favorite sites below.

AA BILTONG
Fullwood Plaza
11229 East Independence Boulevard
(Highway 74)
Matthews, NC 28105
888-532-1433
www.lekker.freeservers.com
Biltong, boerewors, and other South African specialties

ALWAYSFRESHFISH.COM
1889 Highway 9, Unit 41
Toms River, NJ 08755
732-349-0518
www.alwaysfreshfish.com
Fresh and frozen seafood, including crayfish, shrimp, lobster, and more

D'ARTAGNAN
280 Wilson Avenue
Newark, NJ 07105
800-DARTAGNAN (327-8246);
973-344-0456
www.dartagnan.com
Foie gras, sausages, smoked delicacies, venison, and organic game and poultry

ETHIOPIANSPICES.COM
3315 Bardstown Road
Louisville, KY 40218
www.ethiopianspices.com
Ethiopian spices and spice blends, shiro, teff, coffee beans, and fresh injera

FRIEDA'S INC.
4465 Corporate Center Drive
Los Alamitos, CA 90720-2561
800-241-1771
www.friedas.com
Exotic fruits and vegetables, fresh and dried chilies

KALUSTYAN'S
123 Lexington Avenue
New York, NY 10016
212-685-3451
www.kalustyans.com
Bulk spices, herbs, teas, coffee, legumes, rice, nuts and seeds, oils, pickles, preserves, banana leaves, chilies, tamarind paste, and many other international ingredients

PENZEY'S SPICES
19300 Janacek Court
Brookfield, WI 53045
800-741-7787
www.penzeys.com
Bulk spices, seasonings, herbs, and spice blends

STARBUCKS COFFEE
Pike Place Market
1912 Pike Place
Seattle, Washington 98101
www.starbucks.com for more locations
Sourcing, roasting, and brewing exceptional coffee from around the globe

T SALON AND EMPORIUM
11 East 20th Street
New York, NY 10003
212-358-0506
www.tsalon.com
Teas from around the globe, including South African rooibos blends

WORLD MERCHANTS
1509 Western Avenue
Seattle, WA 98101
206-682-7274
www.worldspice.com
Spices and spice blends, herbs, dried chilies, and teas

INDEX

DISCOVERY OF A CONTINENT